# SPECTACULAR HOMES
## of London

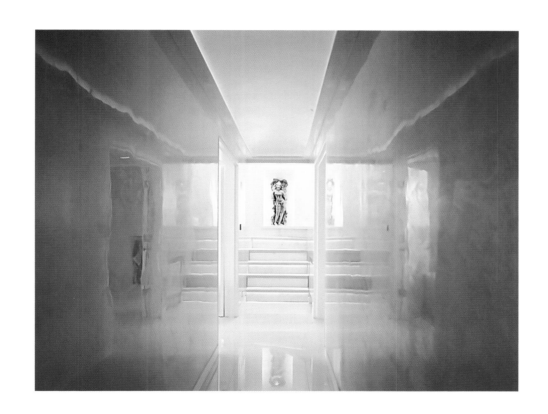

**AN EXCLUSIVE SHOWCASE OF LONDON'S FINEST DESIGNERS**

Published by

# PANACHE
PANACHE PARTNERS EUROPE LTD

1424 Gables Court
Plano, TX 75075
469.246.6060
Fax: 469.246.6062
www.panache.com

Publishers: Brian G. Carabet and John A. Shand

Printed in Malaysia

Distributed by RIBA
020 7496 8364

Distributed by IPG
800.748.5439

PUBLISHER'S DATA

*Spectacular Homes of London*

Library of Congress Control Number: 2008932768

ISBN 13: 978-1-933415-70-3
ISBN 10: 1-933415-70-3

First Printing 2008

10 9 8 7 6 5 4 3 2 1

Previous Page: *Annabella Nassetti Ltd, page 131*

Right: *Intarya Ltd, page 87*

Panache Partners, LLC, is dedicated to the restoration and conservation
of the environment. Our books are manufactured using paper from mills
certified to derive their products from environmentally managed forests.
We are committed to continued investigation of alternative paper
products and environmentally responsible manufacturing processes to
ensure the preservation of our fragile planet.

# SPECTACULAR HOMES
## of London

### AN EXCLUSIVE SHOWCASE OF LONDON'S FINEST DESIGNERS

# FOREWORD

*Spectacular Homes of London* is a celebration of the amazingly colourful variety of work offered by London-based interior designers, and is also a must-have compendium of text and telling photography, guiding potential clients towards the decorator who will best suit their tastes.

To stroll along any busy London shopping street, catching the rich mix of languages spoken by passers-by, is to confirm the capital's status as a sophisticated international city. No wonder culture-hungry and elite business communities, drawn by its magnetism, have flocked from all over the globe to own property in our delightful squares, terraces and apartment buildings. These swanky and savvy people tend to have been everywhere, seen it all and to know their own minds: they demand the highest degree of quality and exclusivity in everything, never more so than in their choice of a designer. The fortunes they bring with them have undoubtedly contributed to the current flourishing of interior design itself in the capital.

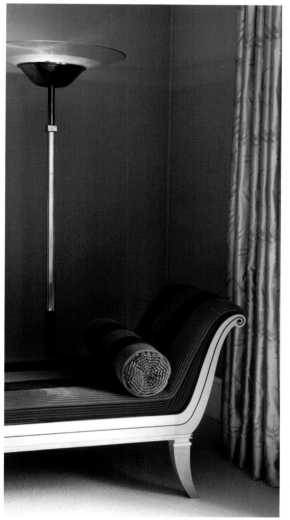

*Gosling, page 105*

*Alidad Ltd, page 15*

*Christina Fallah Designs Ltd, page 95*

*Nicky Dobree Interior Design Ltd, page 75*

Of course, there is a lot more to being a successful decorator than having great taste. Apart from relieving their clients from all the stresses of making a home, these creative professionals have spent years sourcing teams of specialist craftspeople to design one-off pieces of furniture, cabinetry, fabrics, carpets and wallpapers to ensure that each of their schemes is unique. Decorators need to be great communicators, too—good vibes with the client are vital when client relationships can last two years or more. It's also a relationship that becomes deeply personal, and interior designers need an ability to interpret dreams with gentle guidance, and a dash of psychology thrown in. It is not surprising that so many client/decorator collaborations blossom into lasting friendships after the job is done, and lead to further export-boosting commissions elsewhere in the world.

London's design talent at the moment has never been greater, outstripping that of New York and Paris. Although not necessarily British themselves, interior designers, too, have been seduced by the infinite possibilities of the capital where such a "can do" attitude thrives. Home-grown or from abroad, established or newcomer, each of them brings individual strengths to the marketplace. You only have to flick through the pages of this book to uncover a never-before-offered breadth of styles: be it traditional, Modernist, colourful, minimal, muted or an eclectic mixture, they spill out in glorious profusion. Can it ever have been so enjoyably simple to choose a decorator?

*Min Hogg*

Min Hogg

Founding Editor, *The World of Interiors*

# INTRODUCTION

Despite a population of more than 7 million people, London still exists more as a cluster of small communities than a sprawling, unified city. This microcosmic quality makes it easy to focus on the capital's residential properties as its very heart, and from the stuccoed terraces of Kensington and Chelsea to the high-rise riverside apartments, some of the finest interiors anywhere are to be seen here.

As befits a city with a global sensibility, London's interior designers and decorators are some of the world's most highly regarded. They have at their disposal wonderful, perfectly proportioned period buildings, exceptional craftspeople who can make their ideas into reality, and, not least, an international clientele whose imagination and enthusiasm match their own creative talents.

The featured designers in this book selected their most extraordinary projects to reflect the full diversity of the city's luxury homes. There is no "London look"—but from the most traditional interior to the most contemporary, each is a perfect marriage of an exceptional space and the people who inhabit it.

*Guy MacNaughton*

Guy MacNaughton

Publisher

*Collett-Zarzycki Ltd, page 63*

*Atlantic Interior Design Ltd, page 49*

*Sibyl Colefax & John Fowler, page 183*

# CONTENTS

Bill Bennette Design Ltd, page 27

Intarya Ltd, page 87

Philippa Thorp Design Ltd, page 207

# LONDON

# ALIDAD
## ALIDAD LTD

With curving cabriole legs, blood-red studded velvet upholstery and a thick slab of snowy marble, Alidad's Augustus console table is a microcosm of his visual world. Rich, dramatic and utterly unlike anything else, this piece has captured many an eye, and a heart, since the designer launched it in 2004—and for most people it's the closest they will get to a man whose waiting list is years, rather than weeks.

The table, a collaborative effort with furniture-maker Thomas Messel, is just one more flourish in a long and thriving career. Persian-born Alidad—no surname, it's just easier that way, he says—came to the UK as a child in 1970, and studied statistics at University College London before finding his feet within the more rarified environment of Sotheby's. He rose to become a director in its Islamic art department, before leaving in 1985 to set up his own business: London's interiors were suffocating under a blanket of chintz at the time, but Alidad's fearless style helped steer them in an altogether more eclectic direction.

With such a background, it's no wonder that he is best-known for a bravura sensibility with textiles, but it would be too easy to pigeonhole him as an exotic, otherwordly decorator. Peel away the opulent layers and there are as many European and Asian influences as there are Middle Eastern ones, and for every show-stopping drawing room or sumptuous master bedroom there is a plainer and more practical kitchen or a child-friendly playroom.

ABOVE:
The drawing room demonstrates eclecticism in its array of antique objects and textiles.
*Photograph by Simon Upton*

FACING PAGE:
The dining room's stunning design draws attention to the Augustus console table, the inaugural piece in Alidad's Velvet Furniture Collection.
*Photograph by Simon Upton*

Linking them all is what Alidad calls "the unsaid", the complete dovetailing of a client's taste with the purpose and function of a room, and the careful balancing of one visual element with another. With a healthy disregard for fashion, each scheme is not just intended to be fit for purpose right now, but also to serve a client's needs one or two decades into the future.

Although it would be quite exhausting to list all the textures that might make up a single scheme—paintings on top of stamped-leather walls, vertical slivers of mirror abutting lacquered cabinetry, antique furniture meeting Persian carpet—the final effect is anything but draining. Look closer, Alidad says, and there are as many plain surfaces as there are patterned ones. A palette broadly based on the time-worn appearance of faded textiles adds a natural integrity and produces the instant sense of belonging that only the very best designers can achieve.

There is much visual guile involved in achieving such effects—not in the sense of creating a two-dimensional space that cannot function as part of a real home, but in the way the eye can be coaxed into thinking somewhere is taller, wider, grander or more harmonious than its dimensions would suggest. It's particularly relevant in London, where perfectly proportioned Georgian and Victorian houses have often been divided and developed into something more awkward. Here, Alidad

ABOVE:
A faux marquetry dressing room connects the master bedroom and bathroom.
*Photograph by Simon Upton*

FACING PAGE:
The morning room's calm ambience is established through the confinement of colours to small facets such as the ottoman and antique cushions.
*Photograph by Simon Upton*

might push the eye upwards with tall screens, or cornicing that cleverly takes up more room on the ceiling than it does on the wall. If a room has a symmetrical skeleton, then the furniture will rarely follow that symmetry: instead, a great deal of thought is put into carefully balancing the volumes of space occupied by individual pieces of furniture.

Alidad maintains that it is precisely because of his lack of formal training that he is able to be so free with his ideas. It is intuition that lets him know, amid the many layers of colour, pattern and texture, when to stop, and when to push for more. Complete immersion in beautiful objects while working at Sotheby's must have helped, of course, and it has certainly made him encyclopaedic about textiles. Two collections of his own designs— one for Pierre Frey based on 13th-15th-century Hispano-Moorish designs, and an embroidered series for Chelsea Textiles with an Ottoman influence—have an authentic feel about them, both in terms of colour and pattern. With dramatic, large-scale master patterns that are complemented by scaled-down companion designs, they are also intended to be as flexible as possible, keeping the modern decorator's needs firmly in mind.

TOP RIGHT:
Layered with an old master painting, the ornate mirror balances the chair, which is covered in 19th-century needlework.
*Photograph by Simon Upton*

BOTTOM RIGHT:
Topped with an 18th-century Portuguese textile, the table is flanked by 17th-century Venetian panels.
*Photograph by Simon Upton*

FACING PAGE:
Faux panelling creates a warm and cosy atmosphere while the oversize bookcase exaggerates the study's volume.
*Photograph by Simon Upton*

Alidad's work is complex and labour-intensive, and by running a small studio in order to maintain creative coherence, he turns away far more work than he takes on. He has started to take a two-tier approach to his business, completely overseeing the bespoke projects while other members of his studio work on a simpler look for those with a mere couple of rooms in need of decoration. Everyone else, meanwhile, will merely have to look on in envy.

ABOVE:
The specially designed bookcase balances the meticulously restored panelled drawing room.
*Photograph by Simon Upton*

FACING PAGE:
Myriad colours and textures harmoniously combine with the 17th-century Flemish tapestry.
*Photograph by Simon Upton*

# SANDRA ANKARCRONA
## COXE DESIGN LTD

Sandra Ankarcrona believes that the best interiors are about pleasure and performance. The former is self-explanatory—and will be instantly understandable to anyone who has stepped into a room of her making—and the latter means that everything works seamlessly, from the smooth, silent slide of a drawer to subtle lighting that illuminates without dazzling.

While Sandra maintains that it is possible to stage-set any space, something she has done for many special charity events, it takes much more to find empirical, elegant solutions that exactly reflect people's lifestyles. "Quiet quality" is Sandra's stated aim—exquisite textiles, a harmony of contrasting textures and a touch of something unexpected.

Equal to her creative talents is Sandra's business acumen—she holds an MBA from Boston University, attended New York's renowned Parsons School of

Design, and was a director of Clinique Laboratories for seven years. Although a native east-coast American, London has been home for the past 25 years, and Sandra's effortlessly grand Kensington house, bought and restored in the early 1980s, makes for an impressive calling card: luxurious but liveable, it's an inviting mix of comfortable furnishings, paintings and objects d'art. Many of Kensington's finest properties have been transformed under Sandra's direction, but Coxe Design is a truly international practice, with projects from Buenos Aires to the Bahamas in addition to a portfolio of shops, restaurants and other commercial spaces.

ABOVE:
Meticulous restoration of architectural detailing provides a backdrop for quirky signature details such as the feather-trimmed curtains and a framed 18th-century Chinese tax collector's suit.
*Photograph by Kiloran Howard*

FACING PAGE:
A 19th-century gouache depicting a hunting scene adds grandeur to the drawing room of this elegant Kensington townhouse.
*Photograph by Robin Matthews*

In London, private homes are invariably historic buildings, and Sandra considers working on them as both a privilege and an education, gaining a deep satisfaction from reinstating the character of a building and making it fit for a new life. She cites the restoration of an important 18th-century townhouse in St James's—including uncovering original Robert Adam ceilings beneath an unsympathetic 1960s' makeover—as a particular professional highlight.

No matter the period or style, Coxe Design aims to understand exactly what people really want from their homes, whether it's a peaceful sanctuary, space for a growing family or the sophisticated site of cocktails for 120. Each interior is adventurous and witty, incorporating surprising touches—a necklace used as a tie-back or an unexpected wood and silver-leaf finish—to great effect, while imaginatively showcasing clients' collections of art and antiques. Her discreet professionalism means that Sandra's clients continually return, as well as recommending her to friends, safe in the knowledge that she can understand and adapt their tastes and lifestyles. The cycle continues: her services are gifted by generous parents to their children, and she now finds herself decorating the homes of those whose teenage dens she designed more than a decade ago.

TOP LEFT:
This Mayfair apartment is a contrast of subtle textures and colours blending together to reflect both the Eastern and Western influence of the residents' international lifestyle.
*Photograph by Kiloran Howard*

BOTTOM LEFT:
The bright contemporary artwork echoes the simple curve of the chairs, and the modern damask walling marries traditional detail in this Holland Park dining room.
*Photograph by Kiloran Howard*

FACING PAGE:
Clever use of mirror maximizes space and light while providing invisible storage. The wool pinstripe fabric adds an unexpected twist to this City banker's Shoreditch apartment.
*Photograph by Kiloran Howard*

# BILL BENNETTE
## BILL BENNETTE DESIGN LTD

He may work on some of the most prestigious and luxurious interior design projects in London, but Bill Bennette has no time for stuffiness or formality. He's seen it all before, though: in the late 1960s he worked at Arthur Sanderson and Sons, where the sales people were kept hidden behind a curtain, waiting to be summoned by a deeply serious receptionist when a customer arrived. Upon setting eyes on Bill, one customer needed a lot of persuading that a male assistant was just as capable of choosing her chintz as a female one: she was soon won over, however, and to his delight, tipped him a pound—about a day-and-a-half's wages.

Interior design seemed like a terribly smart and glamorous profession to the teenage Bill, who came to London from his native South Africa determined to learn his trade. He swiftly moved on from Sanderson to Charles Hammond on Sloane Street, and has been on an upward trajectory ever since. He has just a trace of a South African accent now, and the capital adopted him long ago as one of its favourite designers.

LEFT:
Bespoke curved seating provides a comfortable space in which to relax. The Rubelli silk curtains are tied high to maximize garden views from this Kensington drawing room.
*Photograph by Edward Hill*

Bill finally escaped the stuffiness of London's more traditional decorating firms when he went to work for John Siddeley, who, despite being a Lord, was both more laid-back and more passionate about interiors than anything Bill had experienced. He describes the clients as very rich, but nice with it—and he has the same take on the members of the international elite for whom he works today.

Nowadays, his clientele usually demand an international look, with a wish-list that means they barely need to leave the house—a gym, spa, pool, media room, nightclub, temperature-controlled garage and hi-tech security are just the start. Bill's job is first to make sure that every space functions beautifully and discreetly, and then to use the very best materials to create a wonderful home that feels personal.

There are still some traces of the tricks he learned at Charles Hammond—subtle and interesting wall finishes, for example—but he has developed a language of luxury all his own. Even listing the raw materials and finishes feels satisfying: Macassar ebony, white onyx, woven silk, stucco lustro. It's not all about surface, however. Bill is adamant that spaces should work from all angles. To that end, there are lots of carefully lit corridors and enfilades

TOP LEFT:
Figured maple was used for this contemporary panelled room. The ribbed vertebrae pilasters are beautifully up-lit to emphasise their texture. Donghia produced the chairs and stools.
*Photograph by Edward Hill*

BOTTOM LEFT:
The inviting bar was made in wenge with horizontal inlaid polished steel. The John Hutton stools provide comfortable seating to enjoy the view of the indoor pool.
*Photograph by Edward Hill*

FACING PAGE LEFT:
Rich saffron and raspberry silk cushions add harmony in the stylish drawing room of this Mayfair townhouse.
*Photograph by Edward Hill*

FACING PAGE RIGHT:
The wrought iron motif of the raspberry silk velvet by Clarence House blends beautifully with the rich stucco lustre walls at the other end of this remarkable room.
*Photograph by Edward Hill*

in his work, carrying the eye from one space to the next. He sources from all over the world, mixing contemporary pieces with antiques: a short course at London's Victoria & Albert Museum, taken soon after he moved to London, has given him a lasting passion for furniture.

Bill maintains that some homeowners want interiors that are for themselves alone, while others are looking for something that will simply astound their friends, and he designs accordingly— grand, formal spaces for those who like to entertain, for example, and softer, more comfortable places for people who just like to feel at home. He favours simple shapes and natural tones, but will occasionally break his own rules with great flair, such as the bright blue suede with which he wrapped the walls of the entertaining area of one London home. That same house, incidentally, was subsequently sold for 35 million pounds, at the time the highest price ever paid for a newly built home in Britain.

The size of his clients' bank balances may have increased, but Bill still has time for all those with whom he has worked over the years, and still sees clients he first knew at Charles Hammond. He says it's no trouble just to visit them for a cup of tea, see what they're up to, and what he can do for them, so he is clearly enduringly informal. For all the multimillion pound super-homes, he modestly maintains it just comes down to "playing house".

LEFT:
Black lacquered walls and a bespoke console table make a dramatic statement in the entrance vestibule of the apartment of an international and well-travelled couple.
*Photograph by Ben Thompson*

FACING PAGE TOP:
The translucent elliptical table defines the casual dining area adjacent to the home's sleek, contemporary kitchen.
*Photograph by Edward Hill*

FACING PAGE BOTTOM:
An oval bath is set under dark green marble in this bay window. The glazing is acid-etched with clear panel lines, obviating the need for blinds.
*Photograph by Ben Thompson*

# CAROLYN BENSON
# RACHEL NIDDRIE
## BENSON STUDIOS LTD

Home should feel like home—a place of sanctuary, say Benson Studios' co-founders Carolyn Benson and Rachel Niddrie. Their intuitive approach to interior design achieves exactly that. Every space in which they work feels warm and inviting, thanks to the pair's keen eye for mixing antique, modern and custom-made pieces to create a distinctive and highly personal design.

The company has swiftly found its feet since its launch in 2004, thanks in part to Carolyn and Rachel's longer professional relationship. They met while both working with the late Victoria Waymouth, Rachel as an interior designer who trained at the Chelsea College of Art and Design, and Carolyn as a specialist in historic buildings restoration. Carolyn learned her trade with the legendary James Smart Restoration, and collaborated closely with Victoria and other designers producing colour schemes, executing specialist

decorative work and working with design concepts. While Carolyn and Rachel bring a complementary aesthetic perspective to each project, their shared background also has practical benefits, such as being able to nurture long-standing relationships with specialist suppliers.

Benson Studios has taken the best of its classic English-style roots and found its own voice with an even freer and more eclectic mix of elements, with a contemporary twist. Each home has a recognisable narrative, anchored by its architectural framework and made personal by the preferences of its owners.

ABOVE:
Impressive paintings and sculptures add to the vivid ambience of this drawing room in west London.
*Photograph by Rachael Smith*

FACING PAGE:
A marble fireplace and built-in bookcases bring cohesion to this drawing room.
*Photograph by Rachael Smith*

Unusual wall finishes, a legacy of Carolyn's background in restoration, are a speciality, including simple distemper, intricate shallow-relief plasterwork or luxurious, fabric wrapped walls.

The handmade elements in each scheme help to subtly assert the individual craftsmanship that goes into each project: a hand-painted floor, or a piece of furniture upholstered in a bespoke artisan weave, lend everything a natural integrity. Carolyn's sister company, Benson Design, makes traditionally tanned leather rugs and flooring that chime in with this ethos. Her self-designed products are versatile and often surprising, coming in sensuous expanses of thick, natural-coloured hide, or playful patterns embroidered black on white—all with a wonderful feel underfoot and a patina that gets better with age.

Carolyn and Rachel enjoy the fact that their workplace is both office and workshop, which gives a good indication of just how hands-on Benson Studios likes to be. They both feel that they have reached an ideal position: a vibrant style that is flexible to suit the needs of any space, talented suppliers to help make it a reality and like-minded clients that are as imaginative and forward-thinking as they are.

TOP AND BOTTOM LEFT:
Intricate woodworking and opulent tiling details were incorporated into this swimming pool in Belgravia.
*Photographs by Rachael Smith*

FACING PAGE LEFT:
A soothing colour palette was chosen for this study in west London.
*Photograph by Rachael Smith*

FACING PAGE RIGHT:
A bright entrance greets homeowners with tile designs, sculptures and other works of art.
*Photograph by Rachael Smith*

# BLANCHARD

Blanchard has just one aim, and it can be summed up in four words: beautiful design that lasts. It's a pretty brief mission statement, and yet, as any interior designer knows, it's as hard to fulfil as it is succinct. The company wants its work to endure well beyond the latest trend, and the furniture and accessories it sources to be fit for years to come.

Many of Diana Blanchard's clients have been working with her for so many years that they can offer a one-line brief and know that she'll fulfil it with the ingenuity and discretion they've come to expect. In fact, so perfectly realised are the results that some clients have even been known to cry with happiness after they've seen their new homes for the first time.

It's a good insight into the close, not to say emotionally attached, relationship that Diana and her team enjoy with clients. More than 15 years after founding Blanchard, she is justifiably delighted with the strong bonds that have been forged with those that patronise the company's services, and says that it is one of the job's greatest rewards.

It's all down to the group dynamic, apparently: Diana has nothing but kind words for the company's designers, who she says are not just exceptionally talented but charming and sympathetic, too. Together they make up an extended family, the closeness and security of which gives Blanchard a particular quality. The reason why clients come back to her is that they know she unfailingly delivers; each home is reliably and stylishly transformed with a minimum of fuss, on time and on budget.

ABOVE AND FACING PAGE:
The eglomisé mirrored panels and constellation mirror create a dynamic reflective detail and highlight the bold yellow tones in this glamorous penthouse.
*Photographs by Iain Kemp*

The company has perfected the classic contemporary look: luxury and modernity but within the context of respect for original spaces and proportions. Everything is built to last, and sustainability is a key idea behind every project. Beautiful natural materials—such as wood, wool, linen and silk—lend an inherent authority to each scheme and are used with great flair to create something that is tranquil, restful and harmonious. Being surrounded by organic materials and handcrafted objects has a grounding effect, believes Diana: such things can act as a subliminal aid to relaxation in themselves. This is an important consideration: since so many of her clients lead fast-moving, international lifestyles, creating a calming and peaceful home has to be at the heart of each project.

Diana's close-knit "family" extends beyond the team that is based in a design studio in the leafy neighbourhood of Primrose Hill: the designers have also built valued long-term relationships with contractors and craftsmen, many of whom are London-based. This microcosm of design, as Diana describes it, works terrifically well, and is fundamental to making everything run smoothly.

TOP LEFT:
The double-height entrance hall has a walnut floor, wrought-iron balustrade with bespoke solid walnut handrail and a magnificent modern Murano glass chandelier.
*Photograph by Iain Kemp*

BOTTOM LEFT:
Rich, exotic colourings against a neutral background give this reception room a warm, elegant atmosphere. The room combines natural tones with sumptuous silks and velvets.
*Photograph by Iain Kemp*

FACING PAGE:
The impressive table, which seats 16, is made from santos rosewood. The modern low-backed chairs are upholstered in nubuck leather.
*Photograph by Iain Kemp*

Bespoke furniture plays an increasingly important role in many projects and Blanchard's skill and success in this area has led to the formation of a sister company—More Blanchard—that sells a small but exquisite range of furniture and lighting. The design studio has always acted as a tantalising showcase for the company's services, but now, full of More Blanchard furniture set against a backdrop of beautiful hand-painted silk walls, it can truly be said to reflect its aesthetic talents.

With a showroom in Dubai now also open for business, Blanchard's approach is attracting an international following, but the company's ethos remains unchanged: at its heart, it is about achieving great things with humour, flair and a genuine joie de vivre. Diana's sights are now set on renovating a French chateau or Italian palazzo—and it is likely to be only a matter of time before someone comes along to fulfil the dream.

RIGHT:
This opulent bathroom has a rich brown colour palette. It features luxurious marron imperial marble, an antique bateau bath and a tranquil water feature.
*Photograph by Iain Kemp*

FACING PAGE TOP:
A stunning antiqued mirrored wall gives a feeling of light and space. The dining chairs are upholstered in a beautiful chenille fabric.
*Photograph by Adam Butler*

FACING PAGE BOTTOM:
Rich, textured fabrics and a gold colour scheme were used to create an elegant look. The dark walnut cabinets and coffee table add contrast and strength.
*Photograph by Adam Butler*

# LOUISE BRADLEY
## LOUISE BRADLEY

Few interior designers enjoy the luxury of a vast showroom to demonstrate their talents—a bolthole boutique, maybe, but not an area large enough to give clients any real idea of what might actually be achieved in their home. Louise Bradley is unusual, then, for she has 8,000 square feet of showroom and studio at her disposal, a space that really can match the ambitions of her finished projects.

Louise's Fulham Road showroom—a complement to her smaller Walton Street and Kings Road premises—allows the full beam of attention to be directed on her own range of furniture. Bespoke pieces have become a signature of her work, to the point where it is increasingly rare for anything to be simply picked out of somebody else's catalogue for a scheme. The chance to own something wonderfully crafted and completely unique has proved a huge pull for clients, and the showroom demonstrates what might be possible, while at the same time makes Louise's signature style more

LEFT:
Comfortable elegance is achieved in a drawing room with two Versailles sofas and a Rubelli silk and wool rug, which are placed alongside contemporary artwork and antiques sourced by Louise Bradley.
*Photograph by Ray Main*

widely available. Not every piece of furniture created for an original scheme translates into something commercially available, of course, partly because many are intended as special one-offs, and Louise wants them to remain so.

Savvy Londoners have long known where to seek out a piece of Louise's style, ever since she opened the Walton Street boutique in 1990. At the time she was a fledgling interior designer, having started out via a well-trodden route—the renovation of her own home to such a high standard that friends, and then friends of friends, asked her to do the same for them. The boutique, she explains, was a way of bringing together some of the wonderful objects that she was discovering on buying trips for private clients: interesting antiques, high-end furniture and covetable decorative objects such as mounted ammonite fossils and robust bronze bowls.

While many of these pieces turn up in Louise's schemes, she doesn't produce a one-size-fits-all look, preferring to let her clients' needs, as well as the fabric and proportions of each home, shape the final look. She and her team of 18 are lucky enough to have as a blank canvas some of the smartest addresses in London, including wonderful historic buildings. Clients tend to be hands-

ABOVE LEFT:
A bespoke commode is accessorized with Maeve horses, polished shagreen boxes and photo frames and a large antiqued panelled mirror.
*Photograph by Ray Main*

ABOVE RIGHT:
Antique silver finish and mirrored baguettes rest beautifully in the bespoke dining table.
*Photograph by Ray Main*

FACING PAGE:
The classically inspired furniture and contemporary styling in a formal dining room in Regents Park is the epitome of the Louise Bradley vision of lasting elegance.
*Photograph by Ray Main*

off, in the sense that they are completely trusting of the finished result, which means that Louise and her team can work with exceptional imaginative freedom. The company runs a turnkey operation, smoothly ensuring that every detail is taken care of, with a minimum of disruption for the client.

The resulting homes are sumptuously comfortable, although Louise is equally concerned with making sure that her interiors are truly aligned with the lifestyle of the people she works for—no off-white sofas in a house with a menagerie of pets, for example. Walls are often left natural and neutral, with a play of interesting textures such as polished plaster, or panels of creamy shagreen. It's a tailored look, with wall-to-wall cabinetry and precision lighting, for instance, softened by colour and pattern in the soft furnishings and decorative accessories.

Louise says she aims to create spaces where the eye can always find something of interest, no matter where it rests. Her way of achieving this, with an innate glamour—the sinuous chandeliers, unusual furniture and pretty antiques—belies the fact that these are immensely robust spaces, too, where every detail has been extensively thought through. Louise and her team put considerable emotional investment into each project and she says that, even when projects have been a couple of years in the making, it's never an anti-climax when she can stand back and admire the finished product. How could it be, when the results look this good?

ABOVE:
Green, purple and damask pillows add colour and texture to the scheme.
*Photograph by Ray Main*

FACING PAGE:
The eclectic mix of contemporary fireplace and antique finished mirrors results in a comfortable family environment.
*Photograph by Ray Main*

# GEORGIA BULMER
# LOUISA KEATING
## ATLANTIC INTERIOR DESIGN LTD

Georgia Bulmer and Louisa Keating have parallel tastes when it comes to design—they often pick out exactly the same fabric or come up with the same idea, completely unaware of the other's choice. They say it still surprises them, but it's a sharp indication of their harmonious working relationship—just one of the secrets of their success.

The pair teamed up in 2006 when Georgia joined Louisa's own studio, Atlantic: the company name is a nod to Louisa's American roots, since she was brought up in Michigan, moving to London in the early 1990s to work in the City. When she realised that design was her true passion, she switched career paths, and hasn't looked back; meanwhile, Georgia studied architectural interior design at the Inchbald School of Design. Their collective experience at the very top end of the interior design world—between them, they have worked for Kelly Hoppen, Lifestyles Interiors and Taylor

Howes—means that, despite their relative youth, they are coolly unfazed by the largest of projects, as well as incredibly well-versed in what will and won't work.

Commissions come almost exclusively via recommendation from existing clients, or from those who have seen Atlantic's work on luxury showhouses, but Louisa and Georgia are keen to stress that there is no formula. They say that their most successful interiors are those where the client takes that leap of faith—the extra push to do something unique and new—and, invariably, people are thrilled with the results.

ABOVE:
A bench decorated with a Bianca Smith contemporary abstract painting is cleverly built into the bespoke joinery.
*Photograph by John Bulmer*

FACING PAGE:
Crisp silk curtains rest gently behind a scroll arm sofa.
*Photograph by John Bulmer*

Atlantic focuses on attention to detail at every level. Perfect proportions—doors, skirting boards, fireplaces—come first: these things may not be immediately obvious when entering a room, says Louisa, and if they are, they're probably not right. Building on this framework, Atlantic has a reputation for beautiful bespoke cabinetry—wall-to-wall joinery in rich finishes, with alcoves and niches for display, storage or lighting. Interesting wall finishes are another recurring feature, from cocooning mocha leather walls in a media room to a luxurious textile-panelled bedroom. Furniture is rarely off-the-peg, either, and contemporary art is sourced or commissioned to bring it all together: it's the build-up of these bespoke touches on every visual layer that results in a harmony of glamour and comfort.

ABOVE:
Set above the fireplace is a stunning contemporary painting; on either side are walnut cabinets with lit niches. A wool and silk rug brings a softness to the room.
*Photograph by John Bulmer*

FACING PAGE TOP:
Dramatic light fixtures complement the room's modern essence with a glass dining table and contemporary artwork.
*Photograph by John Bulmer*

FACING PAGE BOTTOM:
A media room with dramatic taupe walls offers a stunning canvas for family photographs. Shimmering purple cushions and a bespoke walnut coffee table upholstered with purple faux-ostrich leather add the perfect touch of colour.
*Photograph by John Bulmer*

Such calm and unhurried interiors might have something to do with where they are conceived: Atlantic's studio is just lovely, stepping right out into Notting Hill's peaceful, leafy Avondale Park, and the company has grown so quickly that they've now expanded into next door. The extra space leaves them free to work on the next phase—an extended team, bigger and better commissions and, not least, more happy clients.

ABOVE:
Adding to the drama of the drawing room, a contemporary art piece sits above a double-width fireplace surround made of limestone. To offset the brightness of the mantel, warm brown and taupe colours are strategically woven into the room.
*Photograph by John Bulmer*

FACING PAGE TOP:
A harmonious blend is found in the kitchen's wenge finish doors, Corian worktop and limestone floor.
*Photograph by John Bulmer*

FACING PAGE BOTTOM LEFT:
A lit recess contains a Moroccan ammonite.
*Photograph by John Bulmer*

FACING PAGE BOTTOM RIGHT:
A stunning mirror-panelled wall is set behind a rose detail and decorative urn.
*Photograph by John Bulmer*

# NINA CAMPBELL
## NINA CAMPBELL LTD

Although best known for the surface of things—in the shape of her vastly successful fabric and wallpaper collections—Nina Campbell's first rule of decorating is to be practical. In fact, it's the only unbreakable rule: if a home doesn't flow logically, if it lacks storage, if the kitchen taps look beautiful but don't quite work the way they should, then everything else is quite pointless. Ruthless functionality leads, and the rest follows naturally.

Thankfully for the general populous, Nina's ideas are not a closely guarded secret: she has been dispensing failsafe advice for years via a series of books that unlocks the mystery of what makes a great interior. They have secured her place as one of the most recognisable interior designers in the world, but the proof of her talent really lies in her continuing work around the globe on both residential and commercial properties. Add to that the twice-yearly

collections of fabric, wallpaper, carpets, furniture, home fragrance, table linen and blankets, and it's apparent that a rock-solid work ethic lies at the heart of it all.

As a born and bred Londoner, Nina perhaps has a special insight into what makes homes in the capital tick. Her Viennese mother gave her the decorating bug as a child: the family hopped from one Belgravia house to another, rearranging the furnishings as they went. At 20, she went to work for John Fowler at Colefax and Fowler. He told her to forget everything she'd

ABOVE:
Artwork of gilded lotus leaves hangs above the fireplace with its rock crystal logs.
*Photograph courtesy of Elements of Design, Cico Books*

FACING PAGE:
To avoid interrupting the design elements, the custom-designed curtains—made with a unique Balzac fabric—hang on Perspex poles and link all the colours within the drawing room.
*Photograph courtesy of Elements of Design, Cico Books*

learned so far and sent her off to help redecorate some of the grandest houses in England. Itching to do things her own way, she set up her own business at 23 and has been leading the pack ever since.

Having inhabited her fair share of houses, Nina recognises that there's an optimum way to live. Rooms are for living in and enjoying, not keeping pristine to show off to friends. The look is one of artless informality, with beautifully balanced textures and colours and a sharp attention to detail. She says that she would never push her signature collections upon a private client, but it would be hard not to want them: her textile designs range from distinctly Francophile flights of fancy featuring colourful parrots on perches, to beautifully toning plain jacquards and bold silk stripes.

With global popularity comes a dizzying schedule that can take in several continents in a matter of days. Americans love Nina, and she loves them back; Middle Eastern clients clamour for the slice of effortless English style she can offer. New people and new places provide her with a constant stream of fresh ideas, but at the end of the day, London is home—and there's no place like it.

LEFT:
In the guest cloakroom, an uneven oval brass basin sits on a Belgian and black slate corner cabinet, for which the paint finish—devised by John Sumpter—is a mixture of silver and gold to pick up the gold leaves in the wallpaper. The almost invisible doors give access to additional storage to complete the black and gold extravaganza.
*Photograph courtesy of Elements of Design, Cico Books*

FACING PAGE:
A door leading to a walk-in cupboard, which runs the length of the house under the eaves, is decorated to blend into the background.
*Photograph courtesy of Elements of Design, Cico Books*

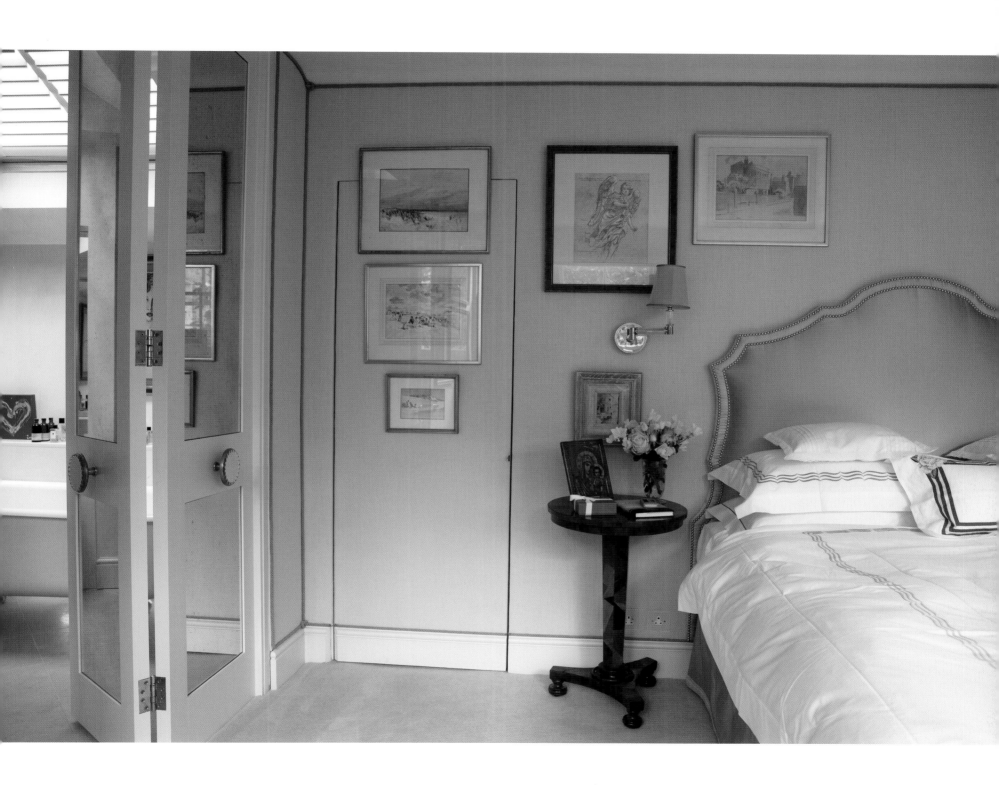

# AUDREY CARDEN
# ELEANORA CUNIETTI
# SARAH CHAMBERS

### CARDEN CUNIETTI LTD

With a roster of rock stars on the books and an exuberant decorating style, Audrey Carden and Eleanora Cunietti were considered the feisty young guns of the interiors world when they first set up in business together in 1996. Today, they've retained the youthful outlook, but the years of experience and wisdom have resulted in the perfect package.

Having originally met through mutual friends, the pair lost touch before finding themselves constantly bumping into each other at antique fairs. Both were working separately as designers, but after a single collaborative project went particularly well, they teamed up permanently. Their friendship endures, and the camaraderie between them sets the company apart—they even live in near-identical Edwardian terraced houses a few streets away from each other. Designer Sarah Chambers came on board as the company's third director in

2006: having given up a high-powered City job to tread a more creative path, she started as an intern, and worked her way up.

Carden Cunietti began life as both a shop and an interiors business. Audrey and Eleanora's Westbourne Park showroom's "anything goes" ethos and mixture of the new and the antique were, back then, pretty groundbreaking. It took a gruelling amount of work to track down the fabulous, the unique and the surprising, but the results spoke for themselves. The shop proved to be the best possible calling card for Carden Cunietti's interior design work,

ABOVE:
Stunning artwork paralleled by sheer curtains and a richly coloured velvet couch adds an elegant touch to this Highgate living room.
*Photograph by Warren Smith*

FACING PAGE:
A converted Victorian schoolhouse uses a variety of earth-toned furniture pieces to divide the room's functions.
*Photograph by James Waddell*

which features the same mix of vintage and modern, seamlessly incorporated into spaces that are both highly finished and satisfyingly functional.

Unusual and interesting decorative objects remain a hallmark of the company's work, from beautiful mercury glass antique chandeliers to sumptuous extra-deep-pile rugs. Carden Cunietti continues to source from all over the world—20th-century furniture from the US, for example, or bespoke cabinetry from the Philippines. A finely honed use of colour and a love of textures and finishes such as leather, cut velvet and gilt—a shimmering luxury pervades all. The company has also developed something of a specialism for designing bathrooms: with boldly grained marble walls, oversize showers and mood-enhancing lighting, they are the proof that glamour and practicality are far from mutually exclusive.

As the UK's interior design sector has grown, so, too, has Carden Cunietti, as have the skilled craftspeople it has worked with since the beginning. The company's clients have never been broader or more numerous, but everyone gets an exclusive and personal service that ensures they'll always be back, whether they're moving from bachelor pad to couple's apartment, buying that first overseas property, or downsizing from family home to retirement retreat.

TOP LEFT:
Pairing various hues of purple within this walnut-panelled sitting room serves to distinguish the space as both luxurious and inviting.
*Photograph by Warren Smith*

BOTTOM LEFT:
An arched entryway and stone floors lead the way from the entrance hall into a Highgate residence's library.
*Photograph by Warren Smith*

FACING PAGE:
A Notting Hill family room is arranged intelligently to facilitate conversation, study and rest.
*Photograph by Warren Smith*

# ANTHONY COLLETT
# ANDRZEJ ZARZYCKI
## COLLETT-ZARZYCKI LTD

At Collett-Zarzycki, nothing succeeds like collaboration. Directors Anthony Collett and Andrzej Zarzycki encourage client participation to inspire a joint vision, which once created, the team of 25 staff members help bring to fruition. Nothing makes them happier than when clients present a new and unique challenge, since it provides an invigorating opportunity to learn and grow.

The company's staff works in a multidisciplinary interlocking fashion across the fields of architecture, interior decorating, furniture design and landscape design. This not only results in a fluid and dynamic creative environment where new skills are continuously learnt, but also makes for an extremely coherent finished product. Such a complete set of in-house talent is rare: Anthony Collett likes to think of it as a 360-degree service.

Collett-Zarzycki has an extremely diverse portfolio of work that takes in some of the most prestigious addresses in London as well as properties all over Europe, the US and the Far East. This international clientele is reflected by Anthony and Andrzej's background: both were born in Zambia, but the pair only met when Andrzej joined Anthony's London practice in the mid-1980s, and they discovered a shared aesthetic. They tend to work together on the initial creative stages of a project, exchanging ideas and eventually coming up with something that belongs to them both.

ABOVE:
A ripple sycamore cabinet and ebonised chaise were designed specifically for a project in Holland Park.
*Photograph by J. Mortimer*

FACING PAGE:
This double-volume space created from two floors provides a dramatic effect in a Kensington residence.
*Photograph by J. Mortimer*

While such diversity results in projects that span the design spectrum, Collett-Zarzycki has no obvious signature style, but rather a signature approach that focuses on extremely high-quality workmanship and sympathy for the innate personality of a building. Chameleon-like, the company can change its colours according to clients' wishes, and be fleet of foot when it comes to adapting to their needs. Its work tends to be classical and symmetrical in its approach but with playful touches and subtle subversion to add warmth and personality.

ABOVE LEFT:
A dressing room is softly illuminated by a combination of natural light and a variety of custom designed fixtures to create a simple but practical look.
*Photograph by Ken Hayden*

ABOVE RIGHT:
An ottoman is situated in front of the fireplace, which is flanked by standard lights designed by Collett-Zarzycki.
*Photograph by Simon Upton*

FACING PAGE:
A John Virtue painting hangs behind a Collett-Zarzycki sofa made from European oak with suede upholstery.
*Photograph by Ken Hayden*

The company feels that it offers a couture service, tailor-made to its clients' needs, and this often means making exquisite bespoke furniture and accessories. These designs rely on a stable of artisans who may be a dying breed in terms of the quality of work they achieve. Collett-Zarzycki feels a strong sense of responsibility to keep these small practices alive, but the dependence is a mutual one: Anthony says that he is only able to design such beautiful things because he knows they will be meticulously made. It's just one more example of the deep respect for others' work and ideas that sets his company apart.

TOP LEFT:
The units of this Mayfair apartment's kitchen were custom designed by Collett-Zarzycki.
*Photograph by J. Mortimer*

BOTTOM LEFT:
Mirrored storage cupboards and integrated air conditioning are features of this bathroom.
*Photograph by Simon Upton*

FACING PAGE:
The drawing room in this Kensington house embraces an air of refined leisure.
*Photograph by Simon Upton*

# PHILIPPA DEVAS
## DEVAS DESIGNS

Philippa Devas has mastered the art of the talking point. A shell-encrusted chandelier; a sharkskin-topped table; a vibrant contemporary painting—it only takes one show-stopping signature piece to create wit, harmony and dynamism within a space she has created. With such lovely distractions to draw the eye, Philippa's work is never dull, nor is it formulaic, and her ideas work just as well in a country house as they do in a penthouse apartment.

Philippa's background is actually more country house than penthouse: before setting up Devas Designs in 1998, she worked with two names synonymous with a traditional English look, Jane Morris at Percy Bass and Chester Jones at Colefax and Fowler. Some time spent at Sotheby's previous to that helped her build up an extensive knowledge of the fine arts. Since going it alone, her style has matured into something distinctive and eclectic that happily mixes the antique and the modern, frequently referencing continental style while still making use of the very best English furniture and craftsmen.

LEFT:
A rare 17th-century Venetian tabletop with base designed by Christopher Clark sits on an antique Heriz carpet surrounded by Regency furniture. Specially painted and gilded pelmets complement the colours of the silk stripe by Claremont. A George III Rococo-period gilt wood mirror hangs above a late-18th-century Tuscan scagliola and marble chimneypiece. A pair of Empire candlesticks sits on either side of the clock.
*Photograph by Andrew Twort*

With an eye for great furniture, Philippa will often go to considerable lengths to source the right piece for a project. She often brings dilapidated antiques back from near-oblivion and also designs her own pieces if she can't find anything just right—her sharkskin-topped table being just one example. French furniture is a particular passion: light and decorative, it fits in perfectly with her style, especially when it is delicately gilded and upholstered.

ABOVE:
A French antique painted cupboard was copied and the pair was positioned on either side of the painted chimneypiece. A 1930s' tole chandelier hangs above a French provincial dining table with chairs acquired from antique markets.
*Photograph by David Beechey*

FACING PAGE TOP:
At the rear of the drawing room, French doors were made to replace a window; a glass bridge was constructed to access the terrace beyond. The large 18th-century Neapolitan marquetry commode on the right is surrounded by a collection of Old Master drawings. The cabinet on the left is late-17th-century Baltic.
*Photograph by Andrew Twort*

FACING PAGE BOTTOM:
The early-17th-century Charles I oak overmantel in the dining room surrounds a specially made stone chimneypiece. The curtains are in blue and silver Fortuny fabric from Claremont and are hung on antiqued brass curtain poles by McKinney & Co. An antique carpet is draped over the table and a late-16th-century Flemish tapestry hangs on the wall.
*Photograph by Andrew Twort*

Heart rates must drop when Philippa's clients finally take possession of their new homes, because they are invariably deeply restful. Natural materials such as muted woods and neutral linens help to create such serenity, as does a limited use of pattern: subtle colour schemes are often suggested by a rug or a painting. Attention to proportion and a respect for the inherent character of a building is the foundation for each project, however, and this is the real secret to each harmonious interior.

Passionate about the fine arts, Philippa says she always pleads with her clients to leave some contingency in the budget for paintings or sculpture. Perfectly chosen paintings—from Old Masters to abstract works—are one of her hallmarks, and thanks to excellent relationships with art dealers she can source the very best. She is fortunate enough to regularly work with clients' existing collections, using her specialist knowledge about lighting and presentation to enhance each work of art's beauty.

LEFT:
The muslin blinds screen the windows while retaining the light. A Chinese table, nickel floor lamp and William Yeoward chair provide a peaceful reading area.
*Photograph by Andrew Twort*

FACING PAGE:
The carpet, made to one of Melissa Wyndham's designs, inspired the room's colours. Chinese figures are displayed in the client's bookcase by Diane Robinson of Inner Space. The Perspex coffee table is from Carew-Jones.
*Photograph by Andrew Twort*

# NICKY DOBREE
## NICKY DOBREE INTERIOR DESIGN LTD

It takes a particularly perceptive designer to interpret a client's dreams from the merest hint of their tastes. Nicky Dobree was once presented with a Dolce & Gabbana coat—leopardskin with a hot pink lining—as a starting point for a brief, and it was duly translated into a sophisticated scheme that exactly encapsulated the grown-up glamour of the garment. Her client, naturally, was thrilled.

It's the perfect example of how Nicky works, with a very high regard for her clients' wishes and above all, a desire to take them to places they never knew they could get to. She sees each project as a wonderful journey, and a chance to enrich people's lives by creating the very best places for them to live, with results that are deeply luxurious and understated.

There's a strong emphasis on the bespoke in Nicky's work—since every space is unique, it often requires a tailor-made solution. She designs and commissions furniture as part of a project, relying on a trusted group of highly talented craftsmen with whom she has worked for years and says she couldn't do without.

LEFT:
Bespoke black lacquer wardrobes and a leopard skin carpet lead through to an en-suite bathroom.
*Photograph by Philip Vile*

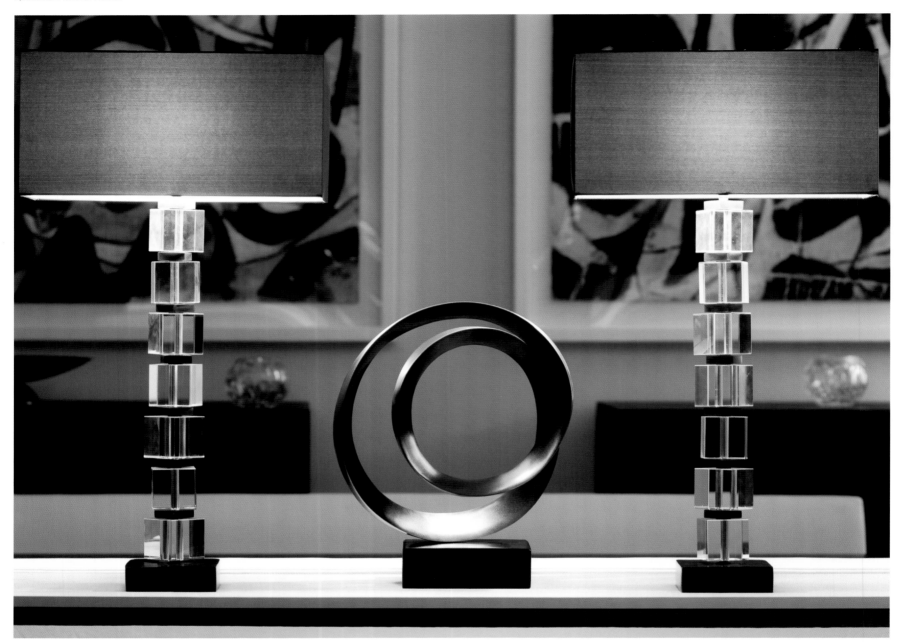

A combination of an innate sense of style and a healthy dose of perfectionism prompted Nicky to train as an interior architect. It led to a seven-year stint with London-based Taylor Howes Designs, where she grew with the company, taking it in new directions with her contemporary aesthetic. She struck out on her own in 2000, and has since built up an international clientele for whom London is often one base of many. Nicky understands only too well the need to feel instantly comfortable, no matter where home is: having grown up in Paris and Vietnam before coming to the UK, she can truly lay claim to global citizenship, and an ongoing love of travel plays a large part in her continually evolving visual sense.

ABOVE:
On a limestone console, a pair of lamps and a contemporary sculpture enhance the symmetry of the room.
*Photograph by Philip Vile*

FACING PAGE TOP:
Silk curtains spanning the whole width of the room create a luxurious and glamorous backdrop in the bedroom.
*Photograph by Philip Vile*

FACING PAGE BOTTOM:
The hall and living room are visually connected with the bedroom.
*Photograph by Philip Vile*

ABOVE:
Clean lines and a muted palette create harmony and balance in this elegant penthouse living room.
*Photograph by Philip Vile*

FACING PAGE TOP:
Furniture is arranged symmetrically to increase the sense of calm and balance.
*Photograph by Philip Vile*

FACING PAGE BOTTOM:
Rich tactile textures such as fabric-lined walls, silk curtains, wool and fur blend together to create a sense of warmth and luxury.
*Photograph by Philip Vile*

Nicky offers a completely customised service, from working with builders on little more than ruins to placing that last treasured possession on the mantel. Getting the flow of the space to work correctly and retaining the soul of the building, are what matter most. Authenticity of place is paramount: every project is considered in the context of its situation, and local materials are often used to create a look that is sympathetic to their surroundings but innovative and unanticipated at the same time.

Equally important is authenticity of personality. Nicky aims for nothing less than a total sense of belonging–a perfect, three-dimensional manifestation of her clients' identities, with all their complexities. By tapping into this unique package of roots, feelings and desires, she creates something that is so perfectly "home" that it seamlessly fits each individual. Her luxurious spaces are full of warmth and life and they invite people to shut away the hustle and bustle of the city and unwind.

Nothing demonstrates this philosophy better than her most challenging project to date, creating a holiday home for her own family in Haute-Savoie in the French Alps. By respecting the original timber and stone framework of the 300-year-old farmhouse, yet introducing her own pared-down contemporary style within, Nicky created something unique in the Alps.

This ultimate retreat caught the imagination of the press–the whole project was filmed for Channel 4's "Grand Designs Abroad"–and Nicky has since gone on to redesign luxury chalets for clients in France, Italy, Switzerland and beyond. Her fluent French and Italian have certainly helped her negotiate through the minefield of cultural and legal subtleties that await anyone building abroad, but as anyone who watched her in action on "Grand Designs" knows, it's her easy, unflappable nature and simple command of exactly what she wants that are the real secrets to her success.

# LUIGI ESPOSITO
## CASA FORMA LTD

Brazilian-born Luigi Esposito first arrived in London in 1996 for a two-month English course, but such is the allure of the city, he has been here ever since. During those first few weeks, he couldn't understand how London's interior designers kept in business: in Brazil, ambitious new buildings are being constructed on every city street, whereas central London was already bursting with wonderful, centuries-old landmarks.

What he didn't take into account, however, was Londoners' healthy appetite for moving house, or for reinventing what they already have; or the influx of potential clients from Russia and the Middle East who have collectively made the capital a world leader in the luxury interiors market. He must have underestimated his own talents, too, because in the few years Luigi has been in the UK he has earned the kind of reputation it has taken others much longer to acquire.

An architect by training, Luigi took an MA in interior design at London Metropolitan University, which led to a post with the Ralph Lauren Home Collection and finally to his own business. His mantra is "functionality"—making each space work as hard as it can to meet someone's needs. It sounds prosaic, but the results tell a different story, since they are as much about knockout furniture and opulent textures as they are about practicalities such as layout and storage.

ABOVE:
Period chairs on a bespoke walnut Versailles floor frame a bronze figure; velvet curtains introduce a contemporary line.
*Photograph by Chris Tubbs*

FACING PAGE:
Walnut panelling frames a glossy maple mirror that is adorned with small silver-leaf balls, reflecting the design of the maple console table.
*Photograph by Barry Murphy Photography*

Casa Forma is run with Faiza Seth, whose business acumen is as accomplished as Luigi's creative one. The two met when Luigi was commissioned by a retailer he was working for at the time to remodel Faiza's Mayfair home: she loved the results so much she became a partner in his company. Faiza's background—at 21, she was running her own apparel business in Hong Kong—has opened up many new possibilities for Casa Forma, including the ability to source products internationally as well as the confidence to make clients from all over the world feel comfortable.

Good interior design doesn't respect geographical boundaries, as Casa Forma's staff will testify. As well as half-Brazilian, half-Italian Luigi, and Faiza, who was born in India and raised in the US, the company's growing team includes designers from Germany, Russia, Italy and Ireland. This cultural melting-pot means that Casa Forma can offer up ideas that could have their roots in one of many design traditions. Luigi says that he is still readily influenced by the things he saw in his youth in Brazil, or travelling in Europe and South America. His work for Ralph Lauren has made a lasting mark, too, and he remains a great admirer of American design: high-end furniture-makers such as Baker and J. Robert Scott make pieces that are not apologetic about scale, fitting right in to the often majestically sized spaces he works with.

LEFT:
The mirrored wall reflects an intimate dining area enveloped by bespoke walnut panelling.
*Photograph by Chris Tubbs*

FACING PAGE:
A selection of Ralph Lauren furniture creates a sophisticated master bedroom.
*Photograph by Michael Crockett*

Luigi confesses he has never really liked the minimalist look because it is the antithesis of comfort and personality. Instead he often focuses on creating a timeless-looking outer shell using panelled walls or neutral shades, and then makes a more flexible space within using a mixture of contemporary furniture—including much that he designs himself—antiques and rich textiles. There's always a certain sparkle, too, with light that plays off polished wood, glass, crystal and metal: it's no surprise that chandeliers are among his favourite things.

Faiza says she asked Luigi to transform her home because he was not merely creative but endlessly patient and helpful, too, qualities that go a long way in the interiors world. Casa Forma prides itself on this personal service and level of attentiveness, but it's the simple desire to improve the way people live that lies at the root of all the company does. To Luigi, nothing is more important than achieving a total sense of belonging—for, as he points out, "your home is your heart."

TOP LEFT:
Strong lines and walls upholstered in suede combine in this fresh and masculine guest bedroom.
*Photograph by Michael Crockett*

BOTTOM LEFT:
Walls upholstered in rich black velvet provide a backdrop for an informal seating area.
*Photograph by Michael Crockett*

FACING PAGE:
A pair of antique Florentine chairs on a black and white marble floor contrast beautifully with the modern entrance hall.
*Photograph by Michael Crockett*

# KAMINI EZRALOW
## INTARYA LTD

London is a great place to be in business, and as a centre of creative excellence, there's no better place to be an interior designer. However, you've never worked at speed until you've done business in Hong Kong, says Intarya's Kamini Ezralow: there, what takes days or weeks in the West can happen overnight. She ought to know, having run interior design companies in no less than three separate continents: it's given her some high expectations, but it also means that she can think on a global scale, taking the best aspects of every location to create a new measure of success.

Although wholly owned by luxury property developer Northacre, Intarya has carved out an exclusive and enviable niche working for private clients. Managing director Kamini and her team of 11 use exactly the same philosophy and methods in all of their work—understatedly elegant interiors that are custom-made in almost every detail, from the layout of the rooms to the joinery, down to the last plump cushion on the sofa.

LEFT:
Ambassadorial splendour was the brief for this ballroom in a Mayfair residence. Architectural details were faithfully restored and treated in a contemporary way—rather than gild the mouldings with gold, they were dusted in key places with distressed platinum. The colours and tones all contribute to the blend of classic and contemporary—the classically inspired furniture is upholstered with fabrics in contemporary textures and colours.
*Photograph by Richard Waite*

The company's designers go to great lengths to make or commission unique pieces, which makes for homes that stimulate every sense. Kamini keeps coming back to the idea of tactility: the silken smoothness of a highly polished veneer, or that feeling when you sink into a chair and realise that it's made of the softest leather. There is also an unstinting attention to detail: no surface or corner is left unconsidered, even if that means leaving it plain or empty.

ABOVE:
The black and white images on the deep chocolate leather-clad wall were carefully selected, scaled and framed to work as a complete collection, while still maintaining a sense of eclectic interest.
*Photograph by Richard Waite*

FACING PAGE TOP:
The bespoke joinery unit is made of walnut—the warm tones and grain complement the scheme and serve as a perfect backdrop to the crispness of the upholstered seating and clean lines of the dining table. Lighting was key to creating an intimate dining experience.
*Photograph by Richard Waite*

FACING PAGE BOTTOM:
As a contemporary interpretation of a classic technique, the walls were silk-wrapped in the sumptuous ivory and gold damask, while the rest of the scheme remained quite calm with tones of ivory. The throw on the bed is a bespoke piece made of wool with satin embroidered flowers.
*Photograph by Richard Waite*

Through its work on Northacre's developments, Intarya has developed a particular skill for reinventing the interiors of historic properties: retaining their wonderful period features, complementing them with superb furniture and joinery, and seamlessly installing the technical mod-cons that modern lifestyles demand. Rather than dutifully recreating period furnishings, designers will add a unique twist: original plaster mouldings dusted with a light platinum finish, rather than gilded, for example, or contemporary textiles used to upholster classically shaped furniture. Huge effort is made to make each show-house feel livable and welcoming, and it pays off: 80 percent of the eventual buyers leave the décor exactly as it is, right down to the art folios on the coffee table.

Having grown up in Hong Kong, Kamini first lived in London when she was studying for her degree, and she has taken a circuitous route to get back to the UK. She discovered a passion for textiles on a sourcing trip to India with her mother, who then owned an interior accessories shop in Hong Kong: after returning to London to complete an interiors postgraduate course at the Inchbald School of Design, she went back to Hong Kong to

TOP RIGHT:
The overscale silk damask wallcovering creates a striking backdrop to the silk velvet chaise with sumptuous, rich cushions in silk and cut velvets, next to which stands a glass floor lamp with bespoke shade.
*Photograph by Richard Waite*

BOTTOM RIGHT:
The bespoke joinery unit follows the lines of the mouldings on the walls and combines materials such as timber, metal and antique mirror. The addition of a sofa and a red ponyskin ottoman completes the sense of a warm, inviting gentleman's study.
*Photograph by Richard Waite*

FACING PAGE:
Design inspiration for this Mayfair residence was derived from the crispness of the white fireplace mantel against the pine panelling, which is a listed feature that could not be altered in any way. The scheme is one of ultimate luxury and tactility with the use of whites, blacks, antique gold, platinum and cushions with embroidery and braids.
*Photograph by Richard Waite*

set up her own business, before following her husband to Los Angeles and starting again from scratch. Northacre then tracked her down all the way across the Atlantic–six years later, and with an impressive portfolio to her name–and so she found herself back in London in 2005.

Kamini's international outlook has also given her an understanding of the cultural sensitivities of working with international clients, as well as a leading edge in terms of sourcing, since she owns a bulging contacts book of suppliers from all corners of the world. Intarya places high importance on honouring and respecting homeowners' wishes, and Kamini points out the added advantage that clients will gain by working with a company under the aegis of a large developer: a razor-sharp attention to budgeting and a keen understanding of the importance of resale value. The ability to be successful in her work–no matter the continent in which she's living–is a testament to her tenacity and business credentials, but with such differing client demands in each city, it shows tremendous flexibility in her creative thinking, too.

TOP LEFT:
The organic, free-form nature of the Picasso prints creates a wonderful balance to the crispness of the sofa and the clean lines of the cushions, while the nickel table lamp and wall sconce add lustre.
*Photograph by Richard Waite*

BOTTOM LEFT:
Sitting against a calm, sensual backdrop of silvers and dove-greys are dramatic bespoke cushions—blue with a silver beaded trim, and mustard with a fern embroidery. The use of mirrors on the bedside table and frame hint at the Art Deco era and exude glamour.
*Photograph by Richard Waite*

FACING PAGE:
The petrol-blue and black dining chairs are set off by the overscale art installation of a Roman head in mosaic. Drama is infused into the space with the use of classic materials and techniques, such as mosaic in a contemporary setting.
*Photograph by Richard Waite*

# CHRISTINA FALLAH
## CHRISTINA FALLAH DESIGNS LTD

When she was a young girl, Christina Fallah was often taken to afternoon tea at the Dorchester Hotel by her grandmother: she remembers being awestruck by the hotel's cultivated grandeur and old-fashioned service, while also being scolded because she couldn't sit still. This little vignette is very telling about the grown-up Christina, because she is still a shameless admirer of beautiful things, but with a little mischief thrown in.

It is personality as much as talent that secures top-end design projects, something of which Christina is sharply aware. She sometimes turns up to that all-important first meeting with a client without her portfolio—if they don't get along on a personal level, what hope is there of a successful working relationship? Her natural vivaciousness usually wins through, and two decades after its establishment, Christina Fallah Designs has the privilege

to work on only the most prestigious assignments—lavish private homes as well as new developments, five-star hotels and luxury yachts.

During a nomadic childhood spent travelling with her Persian mother and grandmother in Paris, Rome and Tehran, Christina soaked up each local culture like a sponge, resulting in a precocious interest in art, architecture and interiors. She name-checks the myriad passions that have shaped her visual sense, from Picasso to I.M. Pei, likening them to a Rolodex in her mind, readily supplying a store of ideas to use on any given project.

ABOVE:
A custom coffee table in sycamore and glass interplays with this penthouse architecture's full-height windows.
*Photograph by Nilu Izadi*

FACING PAGE:
The off-white panelling and frieze work in this formal drawing room create the perfect backdrop for the contrasting colour scheme of the burnt orange curtains and warm tones of the timber floor and furniture.
*Photograph by Nilu Izadi*

Although her inspirations may be abundant, one of Christina's mottos is "less is more," and this clearly shows in her work. Clients' needs vary greatly, but the sharp-eyed will spot a few understated recurring motifs, including the use of concealed doors or elegant grey skirting-boards. Pattern is often used sparingly in favour of layers of texture in a colour palette appropriate to each project, as well as luxurious textiles and striking silhouettes.

Christina says that there is nothing more beautiful than a home that looks effortless—even though it may have taken many months to create—and stresses the importance of sourcing objects from many different places to avoid a look that is recognizable or mainstream. The secret, according to Christina, is to work in items from collections that wouldn't necessarily be associated with a specific look or design.

Wonderful lighting is another of Christina's hallmarks, and here she works in partnership with her husband John, a lighting designer who runs his business, Lightplan, hand-in-hand with hers from the same premises. In their design projects together, light is much more than something that sets the mood: it's more like a fourth dimension, lending an ethereal effect to Christina's interiors. An intricately lit bookcase or architrave, or a wash of light to highlight a polished plaster wall, help to define the space as well as create focus, balance and mood.

ABOVE LEFT:
Soft tones of beige and white, a hint of lilac and accents in chocolate brown grace the guestroom. The dominant pattern in this neutral space is the horizontal stripes inspired by the Renaissance.
*Photograph by Nilu Izadi*

ABOVE RIGHT:
The living room's William Morris listed ceiling, which is lit with a string system, playfully mixes contemporary with historical. James Nares artwork gives movement and colour to the rigid lines of the contemporary furniture.
*Photograph by Nilu Izadi*

FACING PAGE:
Adjacent to the main living room is a smaller intimate dining room: the two spaces are linked by a similar palette and finishes. The lighting is imaginatively concealed behind large-scale wall niches, and also cascades over the dining table.
*Photograph by Nilu Izadi*

These complex features require significant technical expertise, but they are nothing compared to the intricacies of Christina Fallah Designs' most innovative interiors. The company has the ability to consistently match the ambitions of the most demanding clients: a gym that turns into a nightclub, an indoor swimming pool with a descending glass cover that acts as a dancefloor, and even a bespoke dressing table with built-in fridge for cooling cosmetics.

These unique creations require precision design skills and imagination in equal measure, and the company's highly technical approach means that it can be fleet of foot as well as wonderfully creative. A sympathetic redesign of Dublin's renowned Shelbourne Hotel took just 10 months from start to finish, for example. All the speed and technical ability in the world is no match for the human touch, however, and that means Christina herself—bursting at the seams with ideas and influences, yet able to listen, empathise and anticipate each client's needs to perfection.

TOP LEFT:
The classic dark-green colour palette of the walls and curtains is offset by white, hard-lined panelling; the chairs are upholstered in white velvet. The mirrors and crystal chandeliers reflect candlelight and overhead lighting within the space.
*Photograph by Nilu Izadi*

BOTTOM LEFT:
Hand-blocked damask on the white velvet chairs, floating glass shelves and concealed cabinet lighting combine for an unmatched ambience.
*Photograph by Nilu Izadi*

FACING PAGE:
The designer's personal kitchen was inspired by a church in Orvieto, Italy. The lighting and tiny silver lines in between the larger two-tone stripes produce a magical effect.
*Photograph by Nilu Izadi*

# CHRISTOPHE GOLLUT

Christophe Gollut's first skill as a decorator is to make a house look like it has been there forever. There are no nods to fashion or fads in his work, best illustrated by the fact that he designed his London home in 1988 and hasn't changed anything since. He doesn't need to: with its rich mix of influences, from Napoleon III to Gustavian style, it's hard to place whether it was created 150 years ago, or yesterday. Christophe jokes that the timelessness of his designs must make him very good value for money, and that it is his clients' mania for moving house that keeps him in business, rather than the need to continually reinvent the same interior.

A Swiss émigré, Christophe came to London to study at the Inchbald School of Design in the late 1960s. He then took over the Fulham Road shop where he still works today, retaining the previous incumbent's name, Alistair Colvin, because he modestly thought it would be easier for Londoners to pronounce and remember. The Swiss connection immediately proved lucrative—one early commission

LEFT:
Stencilled wallpaper in the dining room and a saffron paint-effect in the drawing room create a sunny atmosphere, regardless of the weather.
*Photograph by Jordi Budo*

saw him decorate the headquarters of a major bank entirely in red lacquer, setting the tone for the colour and drama that have been his signature ever since.

Colour is important to Christophe, especially in his work in the UK, he says, where something is often needed to warm up the natural light. He is adamantly opposed to the uniform taupes and greys that he sees as the calling cards of contemporary decorating, although that's not to say that subtlety and neutrality are absent from his work—lime-washed wooden floors and cool-hued Scandinavian furniture are two recurring themes, for example.

Textiles play a vital role, too, as the floor-to-ceiling shelves of sample books in Christophe's shop demonstrate. He often uses fabrics in muted colours to conjure up a timeless feel, but never in huge swathes: the look is rich and textural but not wilfully excessive.

For someone who claims to do little research into historical styles, Christophe has a gift for mixing up objects from all eras to make a coherent whole. He looks for things that will create a dialogue with one another, often using a single conversation piece to add mystery or humour—such as the framed centrepiece he created from an exotic wedding dress belonging to a client's grandmother.

More than anything, Christophe's interiors are about overall mood, not individual pieces. He says he takes his cue from the ultimate creator of dramatic spaces, the late Italian decorator Renzo Mongiardino, who claimed that his work was not about decorating a room, but creating atmosphere. Using this benchmark, Christophe succeeds at every turn.

ABOVE:
Most London flats only have a narrow corridor, so the entrance hall was carved out of three existing rooms to create the illusion of more space. A walnut wood-effect on the walls, and bands of stamped leather with a French marble fireplace, add to a rich glowing welcome.
*Photograph by Jordi Budo*

FACING PAGE TOP:
Space is maximised in the opulent master bedroom. An impressive empire armoire has been fitted and built expressly for the room to create much-needed cupboard space. The walls are upholstered in striped material that is also applied to the eave over the bed; a coronet-shaped chandelier completes the effect.
*Photograph by Jordi Budo*

FACING PAGE BOTTOM:
Peacock green lacquer paint, vinyl marmoleum floors and mirrored walls address the gym in a graceful simplicity. A handmade mosaic from Lebanon rests inside the columns.
*Photograph by Jordi Budo*

# TIM GOSLING
## GOSLING

Furniture designer Tim Gosling wonders how history will view his work, because it's going to seem strangely at odds with the throwaway fashion in which most people furnish their homes today. Built to last—aesthetically as well as structurally—and created by cabinet-makers with knowledge and skills that have only just survived into the 21st century, Gosling's furniture might be an anomaly, but it's a rather splendid one.

In fact, Gosling is part of a new wave of interest in truly bespoke design, as those at the very top seek unique surroundings that fit like a glove to their tastes and lifestyle. Tim expects his work to be around in two or three hundred years, and he is both humbled by the thought and extremely grateful for the opportunity. Everything is a one-off, and that's where the excitement lies: it's also time-consuming and incredibly hard work. Just one intricate mirror took one craftsman a year to hand carve and gild—so there's no room for any standard short of perfection.

Each piece is as stylistically varied as the individual client: it may echo the streamlined glamour of the 1940s, or draw on the more fanciful designs of Thomas Chippendale, but at its heart is an intelligent sense of proportion and the highest quality of workmanship.

Wood has a personality, says Tim, and there are always new ways in which it can be used to create mood and movement. Burr ash says something different to walnut; sycamore has a distinct character to rosewood: mix in contrasting materials such as nickel inlays, calfskin vellum and high-sheen lacquer, and the possibilities become even more exciting.

ABOVE:
A late-19th-century French vase sits atop the Gosling-designed fireplace, which was inspired by the Karnak temple.
*Photograph by Ray Main*

FACING PAGE:
The dining room's table and chairs are mahogany, as is the floor border that houses recessed lighting and wraps around the room. Based on the Parthenon, the frieze is hand-painted and gilded.
*Photograph by Ray Main*

Tim is fascinated by these subtleties, as he is the nuances of historical design and the way that shapes, surfaces and motifs can have many layers of influence at work. Much of his work is architectural in character: historic buildings provide both a stylistic influence and a physical framework, since many schemes and individual pieces are created for listed buildings.

All is rooted in Tim's exceptional draughtsmanship: he and fellow designers Philip Sturdy and Photis Photi create beautiful watercolours and images of finally realised pieces of furniture or rooms that are works of art in themselves: they have even been framed and hung by clients. Tim's ability to sketch ideas at great speed—often in front of client's eyes, which is wonderful to witness—is a hangover from his training as a theatre designer, when he would need to quickly make his ideas clear to a director or actor. It's not the only thing to have made the crossing from one career to another, for every piece of furniture is imbued with its own sense of drama.

RIGHT:
Standing 13 feet tall, the four-poster bed is made of mahogany and inlaid with silver. The painting depicts a view toward Blackfriars Bridge in late-18th-century London.
*Photograph by Ray Main*

FACING PAGE:
Painted imperial purple, the walls of the drawing room feature architectural engravings and David Robert's work. The painting above the fireplace is a copy of *The Lament of Icarus* by Herbert Draper.
*Photograph by Ray Main*

The difference, of course, is that while theatre sets are designed to be seen at a distance, Gosling's furniture is so beautifully made that it repays exceptionally close scrutiny. Tim developed this sense of uncompromising quality over 20 years in the industry and takes particular pride in the fact that all his furniture is British made.

While entirely capable of lightness and informality, Gosling's style naturally lends itself to formal spaces such as drawing rooms, home offices, company boardrooms and libraries. The company has seen a resurgence in demand for the last of these, and Tim and his team revel in the complexity of designing the perfect library—a marriage of precision joinery, directional lighting and his clients' wonderful collections of museum-quality books and artefacts.

Gosling's passion for the product is its propulsion: that, and the knowledge that people will still be admiring its pieces for generations to come.

LEFT:
Made of English sycamore with inlays of ebony, the chaise longue is covered in fabric from Zimmer & Rohde. The original 1940 lamp from Paris illuminates the space.
*Photograph by Ray Main*

FACING PAGE TOP:
The walnut library has inlays of mother-of-pearl, ebony, satinwood and holly. Eglomise panels are situated behind the columns, which are all topped with hand-gilded capitals.
*Photograph by Ray Main*

FACING PAGE BOTTOM LEFT:
Recessed lighting is a feature of the library's columns.
*Photograph by Ray Main*

FACING PAGE BOTTOM RIGHT:
The top inscriptions are ebony with mother-of-pearl inlays.
*Photograph by Ray Main*

# ODILE GRANTER
## GRANTER INTERIORS

For design inspiration, Odile Granter looks to no less a building than the Pantheon in Rome. Like the Eternal City's enduring landmark, there are some principles of design—simplicity, ingenuity and exquisite proportion—that are as relevant today as they were 2,000 years ago: they trickle all the way down to a Victorian townhouse or a steel and glass high-rise.

Having grown up in Rome, it's little wonder that Odile is infused with the idea of simple beauty being able to create happiness. Her work lacks gimmicks or fuss, instead focussing on discreet luxury that will last, and harmony from the outside in. A dynamic clientele come to her for sleek, high-quality interiors that maintain a classical feel, but still feel like a modern home.

Flexibility is a key theme, particularly in London townhouses where rooms frequently have to fulfil many purposes. With cleverly concealed technology and good space planning, an elegant dressing room can also function as a snug for watching television, a home office or a quiet place to settle down with a book.

LEFT:
A London townhouse drawing room is decorated with contemporary lacquer and chrome furniture and an Italian 1950s' Venini glass chandelier, creating a comfortable yet impressive space for entertaining.
*Photograph by Tom Scott*

Simple, clean-lined furniture ensures that these multifunctional spaces do not crowd each other, while intelligent lighting adjusts the atmosphere at the press of a button.

The depth of thought that goes into maximising every space springs in part from Odile's commercial background. After studying at the Inchbald School of Design, she worked for an architectural firm designing high-end hotels—large projects that required rigorous organisational skills as well as creative flair. It instilled a discipline that has been carried forward into her residential work, as well as helping to shape her style towards a more refined contemporary look.

After working for a couple of other interior designers, Odile set up in business on her own in 2000, with her first solo project, a signature London apartment designed by an architect from Foster + Partners, setting the scene for the distinguished work to come. Private homes have been her company's speciality ever since, and working on them marries all her talents: a prodigious work ethic combined with the ability to source the very best materials and incorporate her clients' unique pieces of furniture or works of art.

Odile and her team of designers and project managers make up Granter Interiors today, and projects are as diverse as a sun-drenched Caribbean villa or a smart Nash terrace fit for family life. The company is supported by a wide range of specialists, from antiques and fine arts experts such as Corfield Morris to audio-visual engineers and experienced builders, who are brought in when needed, meaning that each assignment can be managed from start to finish.

ABOVE:
The master bedroom exudes timeless elegance and understated luxury: interesting textures, from the wool paisley curtains, Japanese-style silk bedspread and painted silver chest, are combined to create interest.
*Photograph by Tom Scott*

FACING PAGE LEFT:
The solid wood painted kitchen has Zimbabwe marble surfaces. The black marble floor, inlaid with diamond-shaped cream limestone, echoes the adjacent hallway of cream limestone with black insets.
*Photograph by Tom Scott*

FACING PAGE RIGHT:
This grand entrance to a Nash terraced house is decorated with refined simplicity, enhanced by the Olafur Eliasson pendant, which casts multicoloured light on the ivory walls at night.
*Photograph by Tom Scott*

Granter Interiors' look takes its cues from the inherent architectural qualities of a building, working to enhance them while fulfilling the needs of its clients. There is a laid-back simplicity in the use of furniture and textiles—unfussy window treatments, for example, or a neutral sofa set off by coloured cushions or throws. A statement piece of furniture in an unexpected finish, or upholstered in a bold fabric, adds something more playful, while a touch of out-and-out luxury such as a silk rug rounds off a sophisticated, sensual layering of textures.

Odile says she absorbs influences from around the world, and is just as attracted to exotic Asian finishes as she is to chic Parisian style or classical Greek detailing. The fellow designers she admires, such as French avant-gardist Andrée Putman, have in common the same disarmingly simple style and reputation for a freethinking reinterpretation of traditional ideas. Above all, Odile believes that working with private clients should be personally enriching for all parties concerned, and that great design should have a lasting impact on quality of life, long after the project is complete.

RIGHT:
An elegant grouping of fine Regency-period furniture, contrasted by a striking contemporary painting, enhances the strong architectural details of this 19th-century room.
*Photograph by Tom Scott*

FACING PAGE TOP:
A first-floor drawing room mixes old and new with great flair; the beautiful 18th-century walnut and marquetry commode was sourced by antiques specialists Corfield Morris.
*Photograph by Granter Interiors*

FACING PAGE BOTTOM:
Displaying a sophisticated design and intelligent use of space, this dressing room is used as a television room for winter evenings and a personal study for late-night work.
*Photograph by Tom Scott*

# LYNNE HUNT
## HUNT HAMILTON ZUCH LTD

ho understands the fine balance between comfort and functionality better than a specialist hotel designer? Lynne Hunt may have made her name creating interiors for the world's finest hotels, but her residential work takes the best of that experience and turns it into something that retains the clever practical touches while tailor-making every last element.

An acute sense of place is common to all of Hunt Hamilton Zuch's work. From a neatly tailored London penthouse apartment to the glamorous Moorish spa of a luxury Spanish hotel, each interior reflects its individual surroundings. If anything else can be said to unite all these culturally harmonious spaces, it is a close attention to detail. Lynne particularly prides herself on the company's ingenious solutions to everyday problems: in a hotel room, work areas are neatly slotted in, even when space is at a premium; there will be glass-fronted drawers, so that guests don't accidentally leave anything behind. For residential properties, homeowners' exacting needs are taken care of, with extra storage space created within bespoke furniture, for example. These clever ideas are not gimmicks, but come from a real understanding of how people behave.

Having attended American schools abroad, it was natural for Lynne to gravitate towards a US college, and so she studied interior design at Brooks College in California. Graduating in 1985, she worked in Hong Kong before settling in London. Hunt Hamilton Zuch was formed in 1993, and counts the capital's most recognisable names, including Claridge's and The Savoy, as former clients, while the residential side of its work continues to thrive.

ABOVE:
Custom fiddleback sycamore panelling with black ebony trim and chrome inlay adorns the living and dining areas of a penthouse apartment.
*Photograph by Matthew Weinreb*

FACING PAGE:
The gracious living space features J. Robert Scott accent tables and Lalique sculptures from the homeowners' collection.
*Photograph by Matthew Weinreb*

Private homes offer the opportunity to create something extra special: working with exceptional art collections, for example, or being able to introduce antiques into a scheme. There is often a multilayered approach to the finish, and always something to attract and interest the eye—leather walls in a cosy library, natural stone floors, or elegant veneered cabinetry. It's important to appreciate the little details of the homeowners' lifestyle, says Lynne: for one central London apartment, for example, she designed a free-standing oval cabinet to complement the oval platters that her client always uses when entertaining.

The space-planning skills needed to create multifunction hotel suites is also carried through into residential spaces, particularly in smaller London homes where every inch counts. Open-plan areas can be broken up by carefully grouped furniture, and hidden storage means everything has a place. It's all meticulously organised, but it still has personality and presence.

Hunt Hamilton Zuch may have the big names on its roster of clients, but it remains resolutely a boutique company. It offers the same personal service to

corporate and private clients alike: this individual approach is very important, and the dedication of Lynne and her small team shows in every room. A new generation of interior designers will develop their careers with this principle in mind, since Lynne regularly lectures on hotel design at the Inchbald School of Design. She is the first to marvel at the youthful enthusiasm of its students, but in the end, there can be no substitute for her own talent and experience.

ABOVE LEFT:
The Smallbone kitchen has polished plaster walls in mauve and black granite flooring and worktops.
*Photograph by Matthew Weinreb*

ABOVE RIGHT:
Biedermeier nightstands and a mirrored wall give a classic feel to a guest bedroom.
*Photograph by Matthew Weinreb*

FACING PAGE TOP:
Spectacular downtown views can be savoured on the balcony or from the comfort of the living room's J. Robert Scott armchair with pouffe and antique Rupert Cavendish armchair.
*Photograph by Matthew Weinreb*

FACING PAGE BOTTOM:
The J. Robert Scott dining table and Essex chairs are complemented by Porta Romana mirrors and custom cabinetry.
*Photograph by Matthew Weinreb*

# CHESTER JONES
## CHESTER JONES LTD

Imperfection is good, according to Chester Jones. A threadbare chair can have a beauty of its own; strange, otherworldly objects can sit beside the finest antique furniture; and the mass-produced can hold its own next to the hand-made. Excellence comes not from a single object, but from the relationship among many objects.

Achieving a spontaneous, artless appearance by leaving things slightly unfinished is an old decorators' trick, but it's rarely accomplished with such aplomb. Chester's interiors live and breathe—existing in the moment, but still managing to embrace all of the history and the hidden stories of a house and its inhabitants. That almost undetectable feeling of incompleteness makes them feel like places of real possibility that will continue to grow and evolve.

If there is a signature style, it is one that looks as if it has been developed over time by several generations, or reflects an individual's evolving tastes. It gets interesting when a client is creatively like-minded, says

LEFT:
This Arts-and-Crafts studio has been filled with an eclectic collection of objects: tribal artefacts, modern pictures and curios, a pair of 1950s' French chairs in cowhide, a Japanese chicken pen functioning as a table and an assortment of Chester Jones furniture.
*Photograph by David Montgomery*

Chester: he clearly has a great appetite for the process of forging a final look as much as the finished product, describing it as a shared intellectual dialogue that flows and changes as new possibilities emerge. It is no surprise that his studio has worked on houses for people who already boast wonderful and eclectic collections, including a number of eminent art and antique dealers.

**ABOVE LEFT:**
The hardwood table is surrounded by a collection of objects and sculpture by Lucio Fontana, Sir Anthony Caro and Jacques Lambert-Rucki.
*Photograph by David Montgomery*

**ABOVE RIGHT:**
A Chester Jones low table and lamp, along with 1950s' French chairs, a Kipinga throwing knife and a drawing by Mimmo Palladino, adorn the corner of the studio.
*Photograph by David Montgomery*

**FACING PAGE:**
The bookcases, chimney piece and dining table designed by Chester Jones are complemented by 1930s' French chairs and a Murano chandelier and Venetian mirror of the same era.
*Photograph by David Montgomery*

There's no trace of a fashionable "luxe" look in Chester's schemes—no cut velvets or metallic-shot silks. Instead, a quieter sense of luxury pervades, with the use of more modest materials that are nonetheless of the highest quality, combined with bespoke furniture, antiques and outstanding contemporary art. This lack of ostentation has its roots in a passion for the mid-century Modernists: clarity of form wins over decorative embellishment every time, and colour schemes tend to nod to the palettes of the 20th-century greats— Mondrian-like red and black, or the brown-paper-and-string tones of a cubist-era Picasso.

Such progressive inspirations belie a much more traditional past: Chester spent several years as the managing director of the ultimate English decorating firm, Colefax and Fowler. He is still occasionally called upon to work on traditional schemes, but clients are increasingly seeking something less formal and grand, and more eclectic. That indefinable mix of old and new is much harder to perfect, but it certainly helps when it is brought to life by a designer with as much creative dynamism and sense of purpose as Chester Jones.

LEFT:
An exquisite 17th-century Spanish table is positioned in front of the library's bay window.
*Photograph by David Montgomery*

FACING PAGE LEFT:
Shutters alone control the amount of light that filters through the remodelled bay window. An 18th-century Chinese chair and Sandy Jones carpet are focal points of the master bedroom.
*Photograph by David Montgomery*

FACING PAGE RIGHT:
A sparely furnished dressing room includes Chinese-inspired wardrobes, a Jean Royere-designed chair and a dressing table by Jacques Dumond.
*Photograph by David Montgomery*

# HUGH LESLIE
## HUGH LESLIE LTD

There's a difference between interior design and mere set-dressing, and Hugh Leslie is definitely a proponent of the former. His interiors have substance and style in equal measure; they are clever and confident, and they work, too.

Born and raised in New Zealand, Hugh came to London in the 1980s. He initially focussed on commercial design work—in these boom years, shops and offices initially seemed like a more exciting prospect than the more traditional direction in which residential interiors appeared to be headed. When he discovered the handful of designers that was doing something new and innovative in people's homes, however, he decided it was time to switch.

An impressive roster of in-house roles followed: first at Sibyl Colefax & John Fowler under Chester Jones, then at John Stefanidis and Mlinaric, Henry & Zervudachi. Hugh returned to work with Chester, by then running his own company, in the 1990s, eventually becoming a director there.

LEFT:
Illustrating the designer's eclectic style, the dining room is furnished with a 17th-century japanned mirror and a Regency breakfast table flanked by Paul Evans display cases containing Delft, oriental and modern ceramics.
*Photograph by Marcus Peel*

Hugh Leslie Ltd was set up in 2003, combining his love of eclecticism and design, and an appreciation of the vital creative contribution that each client can bring to a project.

With the constant objectives of both comfort and liveability, the company takes on projects from start to finish, including complex interior architecture and complete project management. It offers a personal service, with open-mindedness a particular strength, says Hugh: he doesn't prescribe what he will and won't do, or stick to one style. He sees himself as a facilitator—someone who interprets, and then realises, his clients' desires.

Hugh is not one for turning back the clock on an architectural space, or fixing it in one era, preferring instead to leave intact the most interesting parts of the past while clearly defining the new. A blend of interesting textures—felt walls, alabaster-topped tables, parchment-fronted drawers—and unpredictable juxtapositions of furniture and objects ensure that the eye is never bored.

Few styles are off-limits, as long as they are in tune with the scheme as a whole, so Modernist aluminium 1970s' furniture is used to breathe new life into a curvy Regency breakfast table, and the clean silhouette of a 1930s' daybed makes a pleasing contrast with a pair of ornate Anglo-Indian chairs. Specially sourced contemporary art and sculpture add vitality and personality.

Despite the exotic origins of some of these pieces, most are bought from London dealers and showrooms. Hugh also designs many pieces himself, often with a brief to incorporate the rigours of modern living—television, audio-visual systems or air conditioning—into clever cabinetry. In fact, he says, he feels lost without a pencil in hand—an indication of the tight rein he has kept on his creative skills, with no sacrifice to quality.

ABOVE:
A tatami-inspired carpet, 1930s' chaise and 19th-century Anglo-Indian ebony armchairs are mixed with modern British paintings and sculptures to elegantly furnish the first-floor drawing room in one of London's finest 18th-century crescents.
*Photograph by Marcus Peel*

ABOVE LEFT:
Complementing the comfortable and stylish sitting room are a Neoclassical chimney piece, a pair of Regency painted open armchairs and a sculpture by Emily Young.
*Photograph by Marcus Peel*

ABOVE RIGHT:
The bright breakfast room combines a custom-designed veneered and lacquered sideboard and table with a Gillian Ayres carpet and Damien Hirst print. Accentuating the space are Swedish ceramics from the 1950s.
*Photograph by Marcus Peel*

# ANNABELLA NASSETTI
## ANNABELLA NASSETTI LTD

For those looking to stretch, pull and manipulate every last morsel of space in their home to its best advantage, Annabella Nassetti should be the interior designer at the top of the list. Her ability to maximise space—not just for the requirements of modern living, but for future saleability, too—has won her many fans. Add in her quirky, personal take on interior finishes and the results are as distinctive as they are beautiful.

Brought up and educated in Milan, Annabella's first love was for industrial design, and her graduate work was nominated for one of Europe's most prestigious design awards, the Milan Trienniale's Compasso D'oro. The accolade encouraged her to seek out new visual perspectives, and prompted a move to London in 1997, where she then pursued a passion for architectural interior design. Now she perfectly combines the two disciplines— detailed thinking about single objects and the way that they work, plus a flair for the bigger picture and the transformation of complete spaces.

Any set of "before and after" photographs of one of Annabella's projects is an indicator of just how great a change she is able to make. After stripping a room down to bare brick and rafters, she will open up the space, and then divide it up in a way that conceals the things that don't need to be seen all the time—televisions, radiators and other storage space, for example. The effect is sleek and seamless, a look that's added to by built-in furniture, recessed lighting and the use of luxurious finishes such as marble, onyx and polished plaster. She has even experimented with using high-shine, super-smooth car paints as a finish. Don't forget to look up, either: ceilings are

ABOVE:
Clean design statements within the architectural space make the interior of this Pimlico home a more interesting and exciting environment to live and entertain in.
*Photograph by Heike Bohnstengel, www.kayenne.net*

FACING PAGE:
Special wall, floor and ceiling finishes have been used to accentuate the architectural details of a South Kensington residence.
*Photograph by Heike Bohnstengel, www.kayenne.net*

rarely flat expanses, and are instead transformed with domes or shallow vaulting, raked with invisible lighting.

These stunning effects take up much time and effort, but they are Annabella's passion, and she is always pushing herself to achieve greater things. Her clients come to her for these innovative ideas, but also because she is reliable—she oversees her own construction teams, so there's no stinting on quality, or builders prematurely losing interest and leaving for the next job. Clients will often consult her prior to buying a property, so that she can offer advice on how viable the space is for transformation: resale value is often an important factor, too, and Annabella says that she always aims to decorate in a way that will not date.

Annabella is the type to wear her heart on her sleeve, and love for her subject infects those around her. Her greatest reward is the satisfaction of her clients and they, in turn, trust her to come up with ever-more brilliant and challenging ideas, and deliver them perfectly.

ABOVE LEFT:
Bespoke furniture was designed to give a unique look, while also helping to maximise the use of space.
*Photograph by Heike Bohnstengel, www.kayenne.net*

ABOVE RIGHT:
Special finishes on curved walls give a dynamic look in the main living area.
*Photograph by Heike Bohnstengel, www.kayenne.net*

FACING PAGE:
Symmetry and perfect preparation make for an elegant space for living and entertaining.
*Photograph by Heike Bohnstengel, www.kayenne.net*

# Cecilia Neal
## MELTONS

A lifelong passion for beautiful things, as well as a measure of good fortune, shaped Cecilia Neal's early design career. She was teaching architectural and art history when an acquaintance asked her to oversee the interior detailing for a brand-new development in Chelsea; that first project's success led to private clients and a new direction that took her away from lecturing and into interior design. Starting in an office on a quiet Mayfair mews, she simply took on the name of the outgoing business, Meltons, because it seemed as good as any other. There happened to be a shop at the front, so she thought she ought to fill it up—unwittingly founding a successful retail business at the same time.

Of course, no one stays at the very top of an industry for 20 years by luck, but Cecilia has a way of making everything seem so natural and effortless that you might be forgiven for thinking that way. Such a reassuring style attracts clients that come back to her again and again, if they ever go away at all. Her invaluable team often act as custodians for the properties on which they have worked over a period of several years, tweaking things here and there or sorting out problems for absent owners.

LEFT:
This panelled drawing room's elegant furniture includes a lacquered cabinet and 19th-century Venetian pedestal.
*Photograph by Andrew Wood*

She is more than just a safe pair of hands though, and several of these ongoing business relationships have naturally turned into friendships.

Cecilia's training in fine arts and her insistence on correct architectural detail informs her work at every step, giving her a rich seam of historical knowledge from which to draw. She regularly writes for magazines about subjects close to her own heart—such as the history of Chinoiserie, Toile de Jouy fabric or how to get period styling just right—and uses her architectural know-how to ensure that the essential character of a room will never be disguised or compromised.

For all this historical knowledge, however, Cecilia is no purist when it comes to style. The ultra-modern often sits happily alongside period features—20th-century paintings mixed with older furniture, or bare-essentials modernity in an 18th-century house—as long as the correct architectural proportions of any home are retained. Cecilia makes the creative process seem effortless, saying she finds that every room tends to tell her what to do, guiding her towards a look that will suit its essential character. Whatever the project, however, a quality finish is paramount, whether that means bringing in lighting and technology specialists, or using the very best materials for which the budget will allow.

LEFT:
A hallway makes a strong design statement by featuring Chinese fretwork doors and Italian strung curtains.
*Photograph by Ray Main*

FACING PAGE:
The walls of this intimate dining room are hand-painted. The black Regency chairs and an unusual kilim create a deeply opulent look.
*Photograph by Ray Main*

Meltons can pull off a restrained, neutral scheme as easily as a vivid, opulent one, yet the latter is closer to Cecilia's heart; with her obvious zeal for pattern and colour, she jokingly claims to have no use for monochrome. Her passions include paint techniques that require the skills of talented artists to carry out—such as Verre Eglomisé, the traditional art of painting on the reverse of a piece of glass, often used as a highly decorative surround for mirrored walls in bathrooms or to add an interesting dimension to a mirrored dining room. Historical textiles are a particular speciality and Meltons often commissions fabrics for special schemes.

Bespoke furniture is another area of expertise—Cecilia will often have a piece remade in exactly the right proportions to suit a particular space. She can regularly be found searching for that elusive piece of furniture at the markets of Paris, Brussels and Lille, and these quirky pieces add a touch of French country chic to what is essentially a very British look. There is an undoubted sense of personal service about Meltons, and Cecilia says that she could never contemplate the idea of taking a less hands-on role with her clients—why take away the best part of the job?

TOP LEFT:
In this modern media room, the pale zebrano cabinets are completely suited to the contemporary styling.
*Photograph by Ray Main*

BOTTOM LEFT:
Comfortable and colourful, the seating area of the media room has "Flowering Quince" fabric for the blind and cushions.
*Photograph by Ray Main*

FACING PAGE:
The striking contrast between the wood used in this bespoke kitchen—white ash frames with burr brown ash panels—is echoed in the brown ash that criss-crosses the floor between the limestone flags.
*Photograph by Andrew Wood*

Cecilia also chooses, designs or commissions everything for her shop, a treasure-trove of elegant furniture and quirky accessories. It has had a loyal following for more than 20 years, and with the launch of a retail website, is now reaching a whole new audience of design-savvy customers. The shop is perhaps best-known for its porcelain, another of Cecilia's great passions: still traditionally manufactured in Stoke-on-Trent or Limoges, her tableware is invariably inspired by 18th-century designs and comes in gorgeous sweetie-like hues that are a feast for the eyes. Cecilia's porcelain designs sum up everything about her: an acute sense of pattern and colour, attention to detail, and above all, a love of history combined with an ability to reinvent it for the future.

TOP RIGHT:
The dining area of a kitchen features 19th-century painted fruitwood chairs and shell niches that display a collection of faience.
*Photograph by Andrew Wood*

BOTTOM RIGHT:
In this library, the warm hues of the cherrywood joinery and parquet floor are picked up by the red and orange striped curtains and blinds, and a fine Mahal rug.
*Photograph by Andrew Wood*

FACING PAGE:
This master bedroom creates a cheerful ambience with pale yellow linen curtains, yellow wallpaper and a chair covered in a duck-egg blue print.
*Photograph by Ray Main*

# ANNA OWENS
## ANNA OWENS DESIGNS LTD

Bespoke design means never having to sit in an uncomfortable chair: when Anna Owens worked with a couple who were wildly different heights, she made two sofas for them—one that would match his tall frame, and one that would suit his more petite wife. This attention to detail epitomises the genuine care for comfort that Anna puts in to each scheme, as well as a keen understanding of how people like to live.

With more than 20 years' experience in her field, it's fair to say that Anna is a safe pair of hands. A mixture of private residential homes and stunning one-off developments shows off her skills in creating calm, restorative places that ooze quality. Some clients have been working with her for years; others are friends of clients, or those who have come to her through seeing her work on high-end developments. It means that there tends to be an established trust between Anna and her customers from the start— important when so much of the process relies on an intimate understanding of lifestyles.

LEFT:
The room's walls are polished plaster and antique mirror. Period features are combined with contemporary furniture and fabrics for a comfortable and stylish look.
*Photograph by Debi Treloar*

Since every space is different, every job is a new challenge, but there are a few recognisable threads that run through all. Organic materials—fabrics that use natural pigments, plain linens, stone and marble—lend an inherent tranquillity, and a neutral shell ensures that the look can easily be changed with new furniture or decorative accessories, without having to start from scratch. These ideas go right back to Anna's first project, remodelling her own flat when she first moved to London in the mid-1980s. She found it so satisfying that she decided to study interior design—and, having doubled her money when she sold her flat a year later, her course at the Inchbald School of Design was entirely funded by this early success.

Following a short time at fabric and wallpaper designers Osborne and Little, Anna set up her own business, which has slowly grown from there. A prestigious early commission for a private polo club, for a major international

family—no brief, no budget, and three weeks to bring it in—transported her into the realm of designing truly luxurious homes. As well as renovating private houses, she has worked closely with one developer, Capital Residential Management, for nearly all her career, their work gathering momentum over the years as they have created ever-more stunning properties together.

ABOVE:
This luxurious master bedroom with gold-leaf walls, bespoke joinery and woven silk carpet is combined with antique mirrors and bronze display cabinets.
*Photograph by Debi Treloar*

FACING PAGE LEFT:
The curved wall in Bisazza glass and gold mosaics disguises the angular features of this difficult space.
*Photograph by Debi Treloar*

FACING PAGE TOP RIGHT:
This contemporary bathtub is combined with classical nickel-plated fittings with concealed lighting.
*Photograph by Debi Treloar*

FACING PAGE BOTTOM RIGHT:
This walnut cabinet has bespoke serpent-shaped joinery, maple inlays and gold serpent handles.
*Photograph by Debi Treloar*

A classical training and background—respect for proportion, and a sympathy for the inherent qualities of a space—shows in her work, but at the same time, though, there is an interesting interplay of scale going on, with the use of oversized, impact-making furniture, for example. Anna's eye for displaying objects to their best advantage helps tremendously when working with existing possessions: she says that she loves to help bring something back to life that a client may have forgotten about, by putting it in a new context. She seeks out specialist help for buying antiques, and also works closely with exclusive galleries, such as Mayfair's Albemarle Gallery, for sourcing and commissioning contemporary art.

An unwillingness to compromise on the things that matter is what sets Anna Owens Designs apart: Anna says that she would think nothing of sending something back 20 times if it wasn't done to her specifications. For the beautiful marble bathrooms that are so often a feature of her work, she always goes to Italy to hand-select the stone. The beautiful results, with wall-to-wall book-matched marble, speak for themselves. Anna has used the same stonemasons for many years, as she has for many of the craftsmen that work on her projects, and this sort of enduring relationship always produces something special.

Anna says she's proud to be "unfashionable"—that is, not out of fashion, but able to see beyond what might work for a year or two, and offer real longevity.

ABOVE:
Book-matched onyx covers the walls and floor in this stunning bathroom.
*Photograph by Debi Treloar*

FACING PAGE TOP:
Contemporary furniture and a glazed screen mix with an original 1960s' root coffee table filled with amber crystals.
*Photograph by Debi Treloar*

FACING PAGE BOTTOM:
The double-height entrance hall with bronze glazed doors is complemented by a collection of vintage Blenko coloured glass on a specially commissioned bronze centre table.
*Photograph by Debi Treloar*

# STEVEN PAYNE
## MAISON AD LTD

Until he re-launched his company as Maison AD in 2005, Steven Payne was one of the design world's best-kept secrets. His high-profile clients might prefer to keep him that way, but now the secret is most definitely out: after 20 years of creating wonderful interiors, it's no longer just those in the know that are tapping in to his talents.

Despite the sideways step into the spotlight, Steven remains discreet and down-to-earth, one of the reasons why his clients love to work with him. He paid his dues early in his career with two intense learning curves: working for Frank Solano at Solano Interior Architecture on some of the most prestigious hotel contracts in the world, followed by a spell with the renowned residential expert John Stefanidis. Steven describes both men as mentors who recognised in him a desire to completely immerse himself in the process, to ask lots of questions and above all, to knuckle down and get on with the job. He looks for exactly the same qualities in his own staff, too.

Lessons learnt under Frank Solano have proved particularly enduring, not least the painstaking drawing practice gained from designing enormous hotels—with their restaurants, spas and vast public areas—in an era when computers could not. The practicality and level of comfort in Maison AD's residential work have an echo in luxury hotels, combined with the truly bespoke personal detailing that is appropriate for a private home.

Under John Stefanidis's tutelage, Steven says he perfected the art of space planning, a discipline he puts at the heart of every project. Framing a view and making space flow naturally from one room to another are key

ABOVE:
In a dining area, secret storage cupboards are dressed with ancient Japanese prints.
*Photograph by Nat Rea*

FACING PAGE:
An eclectic mix of 20th-century antique and modern furniture sits well under this galleried walkway.
*Photograph by Nat Rea*

considerations, and so too is creating focal points such as a piece of sculpture or an exquisitely made piece of furniture that aims to stop people in their tracks. As a result, his interiors make great places to explore as well as to find sanctuary.

For all his experience on commercial projects, Steven has a natural sense of the way people want to spend time in their own homes. Maison AD's use of subtle detailing, great lighting and bespoke storage always makes the most of every inch. Steven particularly relishes the planning challenge of complex, intimate spaces such as dressing rooms—where every handbag, pair of shoes and cashmere cardigan are safely accounted for. Bathrooms are another area of expertise: he seems to have perfected the art of making spaces that are clean without being clinical, which fulfil a multitude of needs within a relatively small space.

TOP RIGHT:
The bookcase defines the space beautifully, and integral mirrored doors allow more formal delineation of the rooms.
*Photograph by Ben Anders*

BOTTOM RIGHT:
This redefined kitchen space makes the most of the light pouring in from the garden, while the circular dining table follows the curve of the exterior wall.
*Photograph by Ben Anders*

FACING PAGE:
The proportions of this open and light living space work exceptionally well with the muted palette accentuated by antiques.
*Photograph by Nat Rea*

The quality of materials used in each project shines through. Timber, metal, marble, glass and textiles are skilfully layered to create a deep sense of luxury, an approach that means even a more neutral scheme can possess movement and interest.

Maison AD designers like to work with their clients rather than for them, examining and discussing every facet of their lives until they can draw out their exact requirements. As a result no two projects look the same, but there is a confidence and sense of order that runs through all of the company's work. Steven confesses to something of an obsession with symmetry and looks to epoch-making classical architects from Borromini to Lutyens for their mastery of space.

TOP LEFT:
The sofa adds an element of informality to this dining area while the chairs and the chandelier maintain the elegance of the room. The modern art piece provides contemporary contrast.
*Photograph by Ben Anders*

BOTTOM LEFT:
An intimate living area is created through the corner sofa arrangement; the table lamps flanking the fireplace mirror the symmetry at the opposite end of the room.
*Photograph by Ben Anders*

FACING PAGE LEFT:
A simply lit statue provides a stunning focal point in this entrance hallway.
*Photograph by Ben Anders*

FACING PAGE RIGHT:
The artwork and classical wall lights lead to a galleried library that overlooks the study.
*Photograph by Nat Rae*

Maison AD is expanding into new territory with the launch of a commercially available furniture range. The company had already gained a reputation for fine, custom-made pieces in its residential work, and Steven is passionate about the furniture he designs as well as the pieces he seeks out for clients. He will often buy an old piece on a speculative basis, if it is well made and possesses the simple silhouette he loves: cleaned-lined furniture of the 1940s is a particular favourite and it's also a look he chooses for his own home.

With a series of high-profile projects already completed—and with plenty more to come—Steven and his team of six have their sights set firmly on the future. Associate offices in Nice and New York are taking the company's work well beyond the UK, and with some prestigious hotel projects coming to the table, Steven is returning to his roots while embracing his reputation for creating inspirational private homes.

TOP RIGHT:
The antiqued glass mirrors on both sides of the fireplace add extra depth to the room and provide an elegant backdrop to the marble and ironwork demi-lune tables.
*Photograph by Ben Anders*

BOTTOM RIGHT:
This city apartment's contemporary dining table, along with the accents of greenery, leads to a cleanly designed living area.
*Photograph by Ben Anders*

FACING PAGE:
Contrasting materials range from ironwork, mirror and timber to wool and leather.
*Photograph by Ben Anders*

# KATHARINE POOLEY
## KATHARINE POOLEY LTD

It says something about Katharine Pooley's work ethic that in a self-confessed "year off", she bought and refurbished four properties, on three different continents. Or that the interior design business that sprang from that same momentous year's work has gone from zero to a dozen staff in less than three years. If her clients can keep up with her, one thing is guaranteed: they are in for a pretty exciting ride.

While the rise of her company may have been enviably swift, the development of Katharine's global mind-set—and corresponding aesthetic tastes—has been more of a slow-burner. A die-hard traveller, she spent 15 years working in banking in Hong Kong before decamping for Singapore for that so-called year off: Asian style has proved an enduring influence, whether it's a simple piece of antique burlwood furniture, or a high-quality silk. In Katharine's interiors schemes, however, these are merely elements of a much bigger mix that selects the best of every style, from many eras. The resulting sophisticated, cosmopolitan spaces are just right for a clientele that is every bit as discerning and well-travelled as she is.

For a window into her world, look no further than the Chelsea boutique that Katharine opened in 2004. Its stock ranges from practical lighting that adapts to almost any scheme, to the irresistibly ornamental—gold-inlaid chopsticks, or lacquered boxes embraced by silver dragons—but the one thing that everything has in common is that Katharine finds everything herself, on sourcing trips that span the globe.

ABOVE:
The clean lines of these cut-glass crystal decanters are reflected beautifully upon an elegantly refined Ralph Lauren bar cabinet.
*Photograph by Andy Hendry*

FACING PAGE:
This Art Deco-inspired drawing room balances classic and contemporary elements to create timeless sophistication.
*Photograph by Andy Hendry*

ABOVE:
A striking contrast between the cream-coloured sofa and dark fireplace defines this modern drawing room.
*Photograph by Barney Mills*

FACING PAGE LEFT:
With its dramatic up-lighting and rich oak floors, the hallway divides the rooms while remaining a functional space.
*Photograph by Andy Hendry*

FACING PAGE RIGHT:
The marble back-lighting and rosewood panelling unify the space and create warmth within this room.
*Photograph by Andy Hendry*

The boutique and interior design service go hand-in-hand, and were conceived more or less at the same time. Following her year of house renovations—in Thailand, Colorado, London and Scotland—friends and acquaintances were so taken by her ideas and tastes that they asked her to source things for their own homes, or work on entire schemes, and the business grew from there.

Those first four properties could not be a better showcase for her adaptability. From the enveloping cosiness of the Colorado ski lodge to the airy tranquillity of the Thai beach villa, they show an acute sensitivity to space, but have a sense of luxury and comfort to unite them. London, says Katharine, is more cosmopolitan, where design can be truly eclectic to echo the sensibilities of a globally minded city: here, a classical gilt chair can meet a modest wooden Buddha in a visual language that is both vibrant and perfectly understood. Each client presents something new, but for someone who thrives on new challenges as much as Katharine, that is a blessing.

ABOVE LEFT:
The entrance epitomises grandeur with its Louis IV chair, Hector Finch lighting and gold detail.
*Photograph by Barnie Mills*

ABOVE RIGHT:
This bespoke dining table creates a romantic focus for the room. The colour scheme is carefully balanced through use of rich rosewood, light blue and cream fabrics, crystal lighting and place settings.
*Photograph by Barnie Mills*

FACING PAGE:
The drawing room achieved a classic elegance through beautifully selected fabrics, soft lighting and luxurious detail.
*Photograph by Barnie Mills*

# PEGGY PRENDEVILLE
## PEGGY PRENDEVILLE INTERIOR DESIGN

As a 1970s' alumna of London College of Furniture, Peggy Prendeville studied interior design when it was far from mainstream, and now, with a long career behind her, it's fair to say that she has covered a lot of professional ground. With every project comes a raft of fresh ideas: she does not believe in repeating a formula. Peggy feels that whether she is designing an interior for a private or a commercial client, the end result should be a space that reflects their sensibility—something they would like to have designed for themselves, if only they knew how. Because she deals with the whole process of creating a building's interior, most of her clients think of her as much an interior architect as designer. Her wide-ranging design skills have been used on numerous housing developments, residential interiors, barn conversions, offices, a college, a hotel and a library.

Longstanding links with developers mean that Peggy has a particularly good perspective on how to present a property at its best. She cut her teeth working in an architectural practice, and it shows in her ability to carve up space for maximum visual effectiveness and practicality, and in the reassuring way that she controls the more fundamental side of the process: dealing with structural engineers, building control and planning permission where required.

Few things faze her, perhaps the legacy of having transformed some real blank canvases—in the 1980s she was at the forefront of the boom to convert the East End's vast warehouse spaces into to chic loft apartments. An elegant but comfortable minimal look has since become something of

ABOVE:
In a Ladbroke Grove house, the new staircase incorporates a recessed, lit handrail. The design includes a hidden drop-down fire curtain to separate the staircase from the living room in the event of a fire.
*Photograph courtesy of Peggy Prendeville Interior Design*

FACING PAGE:
The altar-end mezzanine in a converted Camberwell church contains a rug custom designed to complement the Missoni fabric on the Saporiti chair. To accent the space, it has a large floor-standing canvas by Graça Pereira Coutinho and a sculpture by Gillian Singer upon a low plinth.
*Photograph courtesy of Peggy Prendeville Interior Design*

a signature, all cleanly tailored spaces and beautiful precision lighting. It's a style that leaves absolutely no room for error or sloppiness, but Peggy thrives on this level of detail.

Her own home, a converted south London chapel resplendent with original ecclesiastical features such as colourful reredos panelling and glittering stained-glass windows, offers a contrast to the blank slates that she professes to prefer in her work. Her versatility is demonstrated by the way she uses glass balustrading, modern art and furniture to create a space in tune with such old features, but imbued with a very contemporary clarity.

Clever ideas for storage are a constant in her work, including lots of space hidden behind wall panels or in those wall cavities that are rarely used. Lighting is crucial for her, too: from internally illuminated display niches to an underlit bed with an ethereal quality. These complex schemes are enhanced by the linear nature of much of the art, furniture and textiles she chooses or designs herself—an architecturally inspired desk, or a coffee table with a smart graphic veneer. She is always aware, though, that these are not just interiors to be looked at, but where people can live and work efficiently.

ABOVE LEFT:
The headboard within a Candy Wharf penthouse's bedroom includes a pull-out shelving unit at either end. Included among the room's clever accessories are a Johnny Egg desk and a plasma television concealed within the foot of the bed.
*Photograph courtesy of Peggy Prendeville Interior Design*

ABOVE RIGHT:
Colour-changing light panels, an underlit bed with highly polished stainless plinth and a bespoke cover and throw by Curtain Magic offer a chic elegance to the bedroom.
*Photograph courtesy of Peggy Prendeville Interior Design*

FACING PAGE LEFT:
In the master bathroom and dressing room of a Hampstead residence, polished plaster walls are flush with a bespoke tumbled marble mosaic border. A stainless steel fire bowl is located beneath the sculpture within the niche.
*Photograph courtesy of Peggy Prendeville Interior Design*

FACING PAGE RIGHT:
A Holland Park residence includes a media unit with a television placed above a modern fireplace. Centred to each floor tile are small recessed floor lights, which run the total length of the living room and adjacent open plan kitchen.
*Photograph courtesy of Peggy Prendeville Interior Design*

# MICHAEL PRIEST
## MICHAEL PRIEST DESIGNS

Despite having been in business for more than 35 years, it's rare to see Michael Priest's work in a glossy magazine or coffee-table book. It's not down to any shyness on his part, because he is the consummate extrovert. Rather it's because his clients are intensely private—their homes are for living in, not for showing off to the wider world.

Transcending fashion, Michael's domain is the English country-house style, dripping in chintz and drenched in sumptuous glamour. Comfortable and easy to live with, he maintains that the look works anywhere, and his clientele all over the world would readily back this up.

He owes his international reputation to Raymond Blanc, whose Manoir aux Quat'Saisons in Oxfordshire he designed in 1983-4 in conjunction with the celebrated chef and his wife. In this relaxed home-from-home, Michael's scheme offered great comfort without distracting from the world-class cuisine on offer. No one had seen anything quite like it—certainly not in a rural hotel, anyway—and private clients soon wanted him to recreate the same atmosphere in their own homes.

As a result of his new fame, Michael set up a showroom and office in Belgravia's Motcomb Street, which became his base for the next two decades. He now divides his time between an office at the Design Centre at Chelsea Harbour—the nucleus for interior design in London—and his home in Buckinghamshire, but says he misses Motcomb Street terribly. It's not hard

ABOVE:
Regal wallpaper covers the inner hall of this grand apartment.
*Photograph by James Mortimer*

FACING PAGE:
This grand drawing room is decorated in the French taste as a salon with embroidered silks and tapestries.
*Photograph by James Mortimer*

to see why: he is all about gentlemanly showmanship, and the showroom was his stage. At Chelsea Harbour he still cuts an unmistakable figure, and after all the exchanging of friendly words with various acquaintances, it's amazing he gets any work done at all.

Daughter Polly runs the practical side of the business, making sure that her father's schemes are realised on time and to budget, and fellow designer Richard Barratt shares the creative workload. Michael also makes use of his son, an antiques dealer, who acts as a permanent scout for wonderful pieces that will complement his style.

Fine furniture nearly always plays a starring role in his interiors, particularly 17th- and 18th-century pieces, and Old Masters are important, too, adding to the stately luxury. Michael has amassed a huge collection of furniture on which to draw, all tucked away in a warehouse just waiting for the right space; like many of his clients, he is a collector himself, of both furniture and British naïve art.

TOP RIGHT:
Gentle tones of soft browns and beiges enhance the dining room. The design was inspired by the 18th-century painted linen that depicts Roman ruins.
*Photograph by James Mortimer*

BOTTOM RIGHT:
Decorated in the English style, this comfortable library was designed to be used in the evenings.
*Photograph by James Mortimer*

FACING PAGE:
The drawing room faces west and captures the evening sun, which shimmers through the plane trees.
*Photograph by James Mortimer*

Michael's interiors have a sense of drama about them, but they are not stage sets: the quality of materials and workmanship means that they are built to last. With patterned wallpapers and paint finishes, ornate window dressings, and acres of gorgeous textiles, each room is a feast for the eyes, and close detailing means that it is hard to get bored of looking or exploring. Furnishings are often overscaled to create an imposing look, although symmetry and an overriding adherence to classical proportion means that nothing ever feels confusing or too lively.

Although aware of the privilege of being able to pick and choose his clients, Michael insists that it's not the big budgets that excite him the most, but people with a shared passion for his style. He'll gladly make a lampshade or a cushion for someone, a practice that in the past has often led to much bigger things, but from the smallest job to the most prestigious, he aims to make his clients feel totally spoilt. Now in his 70s, Michael shows no sign of slowing down, but if he ever does decide to retire, interior design will be less colourful—in every sense.

TOP LEFT:
The master bedroom's French Mauny wallcovering provides a wonderful background for important artwork and a Chippendale mirror.
*Photograph by James Mortimer*

BOTTOM LEFT:
A lovely Henry Pickering painting hangs above the 18th-century French marble fireplace.
*Photograph by James Mortimer*

FACING PAGE:
Morning sun floods the octagonal-shaped, French-inspired bedroom.
*Photograph by James Mortimer*

# APRIL RUSSELL
## APRIL RUSSELL DESIGNS LTD

To enter April Russell's world is to be welcomed into a world of calmness. Her first rule of design is to keep everything simple, and then, like a painting, build layer upon layer to reflect the character and lifestyle of her clients.

April says that design has always been in her soul. Brought up in New York, and the youngest of four children, she grew up spending a great deal of time with her parents. They frequently entertained at home, and she quickly came to appreciate the skills needed to create a warm and welcoming interior. The fabulous homes she visited as a child didn't go unnoticed either, and to this day she sees the world with eyes wide open, unwilling to miss an unusual feature or tiny detail.

In the late 1970s, April came to London to cultivate her eye still further. After a year training at the Inchbald School of Design and Sotheby's, she travelled extensively in Europe, saturating herself in the fine and decorative arts, before settling back in London, where she has been based ever since.

April overhauled her first London house—an investment property in Chester Square—in 1990. Her friend Piers von Westenholz picked up on her skill as a project manager and designer, and invited her to work for the interior design side of his business. She shone in her new role, and subsequently went on to work for Jane Morris at Percy Bass for seven years before setting off on her own.

ABOVE:
Thoughtful details greatly enhance the ambience of the open kitchen and dining area.
*Photograph by Magdalena Plewa*

FACING PAGE:
With furniture made specially by Christian Liaigre and upholstery by George Smith, the comfortable seating area is an ideal place for reading and conversation.
*Photograph by Magdalena Plewa*

By concentrating on five or six projects a year, April offers a boutique, personal service. Her look is luxurious but not pretentious, and everything appears as if it has been put together effortlessly. She has a light but sure touch, creating schemes of great subtlety by using understated paint finishes and beautifully crafted contemporary furniture, for example. Art is a great passion for her, and the paintings she chooses always add that extra dimension, bringing everything to life.

April wants to remain true both to herself and to her clients, which means coming up with something new, rather than slavishly treading the same old path. She says that interiors are like gardens: they grow. Unlike the designers who create a scheme they expect to be timeless and immutable, she likes to add, subtract and adjust. Her clients' needs are always evolving, and so should the way they live.

ABOVE LEFT:
A collection of witty decorative art hangs in the guest cloakroom of a refurbished Chelsea flat. The soft texture of the walls blends with the blue Moleanos stone. The bronze crab reminds the clients of a trip to Vamizi Island off Mozambique.
*Photograph by Magdalena Plewa*

ABOVE RIGHT:
The mid-20th-century French table and chairs are used for frequent backgammon and card games; the bronze Italian nutcracker and French sculpture are of the same period. French artist André Marchand created the painting, which has been nicknamed Maud.
*Photograph by Magdalena Plewa*

FACING PAGE:
Once a large master bedroom and bathroom, the kitchen and dining area are infused with natural light. The table and benches are custom Christian Liaigre, while the useful display unit was bought at an antique shop in Pimlico. Mathers and Hirst fabricated the kitchen units, which have honed Nero Zimbabwe worktops.
*Photograph by Magdalena Plewa*

# STEPHEN RYAN
## STEPHEN RYAN DESIGN & DECORATION

Stephen Ryan's corporate logo—a sober classical obelisk flanked on either side by a flash of fuchsia and orange—manages to pull off the difficult trick of appearing both conservative and opulent at the same time. It reflects his company's interiors, too, where thoughtfulness and order come from the same well-spring as colour, texture and wit.

Stephen admits that he has a classical, conservative side, yet sometimes has to be reigned in by members of his team when he proposes a design that's a little too outlandish for certain clients. He is known for a fearless use of bright colour, but that doesn't do his work justice: his bespoke range of furniture, for example, is full of architectural pieces, among them a mirror influenced by a lintel on a Palladian villa and a Neoclassical sofa inspired by Regency designer Thomas Hope. Similarly, there is nothing frivolous about the rigorous quality of the materials used in every project,

or the exacting, tailor-made solution, with a thorough attention to detail, that every client can expect.

Boldness, rather than brightness, is the real thread that runs through every project. Stephen speaks a lot about being brave—whether that refers to clients, whom he is always guiding a little out of their comfort zone in order to achieve their dreams, or his own confidence in being able to mix up textures, patterns and objects from all over the world and make it work. His look is striking but not showy, with proportion and function given every bit as much weight as surface detail.

ABOVE:
The Parisian raffia wallcovering punctuates Diane Kaufman's *Palette Nude*. Chinese vases sit on top of an antique shell chest from Ile St. Louis, Paris.
*Photograph by James Balston*

FACING PAGE:
In the reception room, *Sea Cow* by Emma Kelly hangs above the J. Robert Scott table with a Joe Tilson ornamental urn. Theodore Alexander chairs and Linley lamps frame the composition.
*Photograph by Nick Pope*

There was little information available about interior design when Stephen had the first idea that he might pursue it as a career, but once he had discovered the books of iconic British decorator David Hicks, he was smitten. Then in his late teens, he even wrote the author a youthful fan letter, to which he never received a reply. Stephen got his recompense just a few years later, while he was working as an in-house designer in the mid-1980s: David Hicks headhunted him to lead his entire creative team. It was a huge leap, from working with a handful of his own staff, to overseeing an internationally recognised design practice with several teams and some enormously demanding projects.

Stephen's aesthetic was in keeping with the David Hicks house style—period furniture upholstered in vivid contemporary textiles, exquisite antiques used side-by-side with modern materials, all used within a fairly strict symmetrical framework—but when the company went into liquidation in 1992, it was time to go it alone. Since then he has worked on many top-end private homes as well as carried out some influential exhibition design. There have

been corporate projects, too, including an opulent refurbishment of The Mandeville Hotel in Marylebone Village: all mirrors and sparkle, with hot pink and orange furniture refined by brown and taupe, it transformed a tired business hotel into the latest haunt of London's chic.

ABOVE:
The sophisticated yet warm ambience of the drawing room is set by antique-style oak parquet de Versailles flooring, wallpaper by Osbourne & Little, bespoke Stephen Ryan chaise longues with cushions covered in Rubelli and Giacometti-style bronze and glass table. Glazed ceramic Deco urns and antique plaster-cast sphynx refinished to bronze further complement the look.
*Photograph by Nick Pope*

FACING PAGE TOP LEFT:
Venetian blinds filter light through the large artist studio windows. Wire-work lamps with pleated organza shades complement the Stephen Ryan-designed Sauvage writing table in chocolate crackle lacquer, leather and bronze.
*Photograph by James Balston*

FACING PAGE BOTTOM LEFT:
Carpeted in a Brussels trellis weave, this master bedroom boasts a pair of Icarus lamps with guinea-fowl shades by Stephen Ryan. The hand-marbleised lambrequin matches the antique Giallo-Rosso chimneypiece. The homeowner's antique wing chair has been reupholstered in "Sellier" by Pierre Frey to complement the antique chimneypiece and Venetian mirror.
*Photograph by Viv Yeo*

FACING PAGE RIGHT:
Boasting three custom Stephen Ryan pieces—a bronze wall decoration, metallic lacquer bookcases and a walnut and bronze writing console—the limestone-floored space is also adorned with bronze and gold tête de Maure standard lamps and wooden South African masks.
*Photograph by Andreas von Einsiedel*

The Holland Park showroom from which Stephen now runs his business is a great place for him to flex his own design skills and exhibit his eclectic tastes: snake-print leather tables and painted and mounted ostrich eggs provide the exotica, while straight-sided lamp-bases and George III-style stone consoles add gravitas. His own home is just around the corner, a converted artist's studio house that is a masterclass in putting together interesting finds from all eras: 17th-century statuary, contemporary paintings and decorative antiques all in harmony.

Despite Stephen having worked in virtually every continent, his style always seems recognisably British. It could be the David Hicks connection, or a respect for history and tradition, but really it comes down to looking at the world with a certain sense of humour. Stephen doesn't take himself too seriously and says that he wants his work to make people smile—not just a nice sentiment but a demonstration of how much he seeks to please his clients, too.

TOP RIGHT:
A brilliant layering of textures and tones, the kitchen has limestone floors, custom cabinetry and Bianco antique granite tops and splashbacks by Mark Wilkinson. Presented on top of polished stainless-steel plinths, the prominent statues of 17th-century St. Jerome and an unknown female in limed oak were the inspiration for the cabinetry. Additional unique features include a recessed plasma television, a Catherine Grandidier light sculpture, and original 1940s' faux-leather dining chairs surrounding an Italian extending table with glass top and stitched leather legs.
*Photograph by James Balston*

BOTTOM RIGHT:
Perspex brackets with velum objets are mounted on the hand-painted walls, which simulate campaign-style Napoleonic swagged fabric. Decorative wooden urns on top of coromandel side tables are positioned on either side of the Knole sofa with blown-glass finials and rust-hued silk damask. The Neoclassical gilded chairs and inlaid wooden gilt centre table are by Maitland-Smith. An unknown Russian's mysterious oil painting anchors the final design.
*Photograph by Viv Yeo*

FACING PAGE LEFT:
Ecru polished plaster walls and velum-wrapped plinths provide a backdrop for the contemporary staircase of steel, wenge and glass with suspended glass sheetwork.
*Photograph by Diana Salevouzkis*

FACING PAGE RIGHT:
The decadent Delos cornice and taffeta walls draw attention to Nicolas Kuligowski's *Bergere* and the Stephen Ryan-designed leather and tweed sofa with bronze legs and cushions by Rubelli. The antique side tables flanking the exquisite sofa were originally from the Dorchester Hotel. Sitting on top of one of the bronzed iron and pin oak side tables from France is what is believed to be an antique, glazed-clay likeness of the Egyptian deity Ra.
*Photograph by Nick Pope*

# SIBYL COLEFAX & JOHN FOWLER

The work of Sibyl Colefax & John Fowler has had a residual impact on how people decorate their houses today, whether they are aware of it or not. The equal partnership of values that have become the decorator's modern mantra—comfort, quality, practicality—may seem incontrovertible, but they were not always held so dear: they are the company's great legacy, and the reason for its continued success.

Today, four directors act as principal decorators—managing director Wendy Nicholls, plus Emma Burns, Philip Hooper and Roger Jones—and lead a team of about 50 staff at 39 Brook Street, the Mayfair premises out of which the company has worked since the Second World War. A fifth director, William Hodgson, oversees the company's architectural and interior design studio, the technical powerhouse that helps to bring each scheme to fruition. The studio can design and produce drawings for everything from the smallest detail to an entire house.

The decorators' diverse creative backgrounds ensure that their skills can be closely matched up to each project—greater architectural input, technical expertise, knowledge of textiles and antiques, or whatever else may be required.

The company may be a considerable operation in terms of size, but for clients it nonetheless feels like an immensely personal service. Projects can take years to evolve, and the principal decorators invite clients to be completely

ABOVE:
An 18th-century os de mouton chair is covered in a linen and silk stripe from Antico Setico Setificio de Fiorentino. The wall sconce is by Hannah Woodhouse and was cast in bronze; Hannah also made the shade from hand-dyed silk. The cushion on the chair is made from an antique Ghanaian textile.
*Photograph by Simon Brown / House & Garden © The Condé Nast Publications Ltd*

FACING PAGE:
The furniture in the drawing room is anchored with a custom-made rug from Farnad Peyman at Oriental Heritage. Upholstered pieces are covered in various Italian textiles complemented with Turkish and African textiles that have been used as cushions, while the antiques are all from the Sibyl Colefax & John Fowler antiques department. The ceramic pots are by Paul Philip. The stone fire surround and low table were made to Philip Hooper's design.
*Photograph by Simon Brown / House & Garden © The Condé Nast Publications Ltd*

immersed in the process. Commissions range worldwide and include private houses in both city and country, yachts, aeroplanes, hotels and offices.

A long, intricate history lies behind the present set-up, beginning when society aesthete Sibyl Colefax set up in business in 1933; she was joined five years later by John Fowler, a decorative painter by trade, but also, as it turned out, a man with both a fantastic eye for colour and an obsession for detail. Sibyl Colefax retired shortly after the war, and the company was taken over by Virginian-born Nancy Lancaster: it is the latter's partnership with John Fowler that effected a sea-change in British interiors, lifting them from a dark, damask gloom into light, useable spaces. Harmoniously arranged furniture, wonderful antiques and a fearless sense of colour characterised

ABOVE:
The clients' own antique furniture is used with modern furniture designed by Sibyl Colefax & John Fowler, a crystal and gilt lamp from Sibyl Colefax & John Fowler with a shade of Fortuny printed cotton, and a specially made carpet by the French manufacturer Cogolin, in which the ground colour reflects the colour of the bed valance.
*Photograph by Andrew Wood © Colefax and Fowler*

FACING PAGE:
The silk tweed curtains, stone floor and wall colour provide an austere backdrop for the clients' art collection, including an Igor Mitoraj sculpture mounted on a plinth designed by Sibyl Colefax & John Fowler, and a Chagall oil painting. A drip-glaze lamp on an Italian console adds colour and an interesting juxtaposition of shape and period.
*Photograph by Andrew Wood © Colefax and Fowler*

this new look, best illustrated in the country house schemes that the two worked on together.

Today, Sibyl Colefax & John Fowler's style has significantly shifted from the style for which it is still best known. There is some frustration among its principal decorators that the public tend to think of the company in terms of chintz and frills, or historically accurate renderings of schemes past, when none of these form the basis of its work, either then or now. Simply put, it is as flexible as the needs of its clients. Contemporary schemes are as much a part of its work as historically rooted ones, but more often than not there is no distinction between past and present—just a glorious mix of wonderful objects, in architecturally designed spaces, that match perfectly with people's lives.

ABOVE:
An existing Japanese garden was the inspiration for a Minka-style house designed for an artist's studio perched over a new carp-filled lake in Hampstead.
*Photograph by Brian Harrison © Colefax and Fowler*

FACING PAGE:
From the reading room in the centre of the studio across to the painting table, views of the Japanese garden are framed by posts, beams and vertical screens. The canvas blinds are reefed on poles using a yachting mechanism. Within, antiques from Sibyl Colefax & John Fowler, a Danish stove and a sisal rug are used with modern garden chairs, which are covered in old French mattress ticking. The Adirondack chairs outside are antiques.
*Photograph by Brian Harrison © Colefax and Fowler*

Nonetheless, such a formidable history means that there is a taut thread running through every scheme—an interest in the craft of decoration, and a commitment to high-quality workmanship. In the company's archives, the staff has an amazing resource at its disposal: it details every design of the past 40 years, as well as many previous schemes that may now only survive as a scrap of textile, a length of intricate braiding or a sketch. Even these fragments can be crucial, say the decorators, not least because they show the original colour schemes that aren't revealed by black and white photography: John Fowler would often place drab, nondescript colours adjacent to incredibly bright tones—raspberry pinks, acid greens—to make them sing out.

ABOVE:
The squid ink-coloured flat emulsion walls of this room make a calm background for the pair of 1950s' low armchairs covered in scarlet wool with black buttoning. A "Mouses Back" sisal is laid on the floor. The Shoji screens were specially made for the bay window in American black walnut and paper.
*Photograph by Simon Upton © Colefax and Fowler*

FACING PAGE:
The walls of this Notting Hill drawing room are papered in a Donghia grasscloth creating a dramatic backdrop for the 20th-century paintings. The Louis XV chair is covered in a Fortuny fabric that imitates a west African textile and is juxtaposed with Art Deco furniture and a modern lamp by Hannah Woodhouse. The wool curtain fabric was custom-dyed to create the correct blackberry colour.
*Photograph by William Waldron @ Achard & Associates*

Just as historical reference was merely a starting point for the company's post-war interiors, today the archives are treated as a jumping-off point, a place to take the best of the past and reinterpret it for the future. Rarely is anything bought off the shelf: the decorators maintain close links with the very best textile and furniture workshops, in the UK and abroad, and a majority of elements in any scheme are either bespoke or antique. Fabrics may be specially woven, printed or dyed; an in-house paint studio creates one-off designs, from hand-painted floors to trompe l'oeil wallcoverings. Specially commissioned paintings or sculpture are essential, too, and clients often discover a passion for patronage that continues long after their homes have been finished.

ABOVE:
The antique Ziegler Mahal carpet, found for the clients at auction and painstakingly cleaned and restored, set the colour scheme for this Belgravia drawing room.
*Photograph by Fritz von der Schulenburg © Colefax and Fowler*

FACING PAGE:
In the same apartment, the sturdy chairs provide comfort in this dual purpose library/dining room.
*Photograph by Fritz von der Schulenburg © Colefax and Fowler*

Equally crucial is the antiques showroom that shares the Brook Street premises with the decorators. Much lauded for its mix of quirky and original pieces, and with a constantly changing rotation of stock, the showroom couldn't offer a more stimulating environment for its work. Tellingly, there is no cut-off date—1970s´ objects can sit happily alongside 18th-century ones—an indication of just how far the decorators cast their net to achieve a genuinely eclectic look.

Adding to this mix are the trappings of 21st-century life: audio-visual technology, security systems, lighting, heating and air conditioning. Tremendous energy goes into ensuring that these modern essentials remain as invisible as possible, and are sensitively incorporated into the interior architecture.

People live in a different manner today than they did even a decade ago, and there is no more reason to stand still now than there would have been 70 years ago. Creating interiors that are suspended in time, or that replicate a past way of life, is not the way that the endlessly inquisitive John Fowler worked, and it would be anathema to Sibyl Colefax & John Fowler's decorators to do it now. Despite the company's tremendous versatility, there are some constants: an unswerving commitment to quality, and a desire to make people's lives better by design.

TOP RIGHT:
The Kingsway sofa by Sibyl Colefax & John Fowler has a relaxed-fitting slip cover in the "Indian Pear" design linen. Italian-strung, unlined, bronze silk taffeta curtains hang over sheer Roman blinds.
*Photograph by Caroline Gavazzi / House & Garden © The Condé Nast Publications Ltd*

BOTTOM RIGHT:
The antique 18th-century birdcage from Sibyl Colefax & John Fowler Antiques, together with the French garden chairs with their beige and white mattress ticking slip covers, create an informal mood in the dining room of this Knightsbridge apartment.
*Photograph by Caroline Gavazzi / House & Garden © The Condé Nast Publications Ltd*

FACING PAGE:
In the seating area of this Kensington bedroom, 19th-century French bookcases conceal the television and provide additional clothes storage.
*Photograph by Simon Upton © The World of Interiors*

# SOANE BRITAIN

The best things in life are worth waiting for, which is why customers purchasing Soane Britain's Jurassic stone lamp have to sit tight for more than three months before they can lay their hands on one. Hand-carved from rare Purbeck marble, each one bears the unique fossilised character of 130 million years of history. It's a piece that sums up the company's ideals: great, timeless design that works in almost any setting, and an unwavering belief that British craftsmanship is the best in the world, and more than worth the wait.

Soane Britain's decorating service grew out of a renowned collection of lighting and architectural furniture that is an established favourite among fellow decorators. It offers uncompromising quality as well as complete flexibility: a beaten-steel table comes topped with leather, slate or marble, for example; a chair can be made in ebonised oak, mahogany, rosewood or walnut; embellishments can be added or subtracted. When co-owners Lulu

Lytle and Christopher Hodsoll were asked to create complete schemes around these customised pieces, Soane Britain's remit expanded to include interior design as well.

Christopher was, in fact, already a decorator of repute, and also shares Lulu's background in antiques, so it's no surprise that historical one-offs sit perfectly alongside the new pieces at Soane Britain's Pimlico Road showroom. The same idiosyncratic mix is applied to its interiors, where antique pieces meet a modern interpretation of the past. As with all the

ABOVE:
The Holland blind—and its hand-painted palm tree—is paired with the generously scaled bergère and plumptious feather and down cushions within the relaxed corner of a sunny sitting room. Hydrangeas fill a 17th-century Tibetan copper bowl sitting on a low bronze table.
*Photograph by James Mortimer*

FACING PAGE:
An office in a London conservatory is separated from the neighbouring room by striped linen curtains providing a relaxed backdrop for an iron desk with a rich tan goatskin top. The ultimate rosewood desk chair is upholstered in a polished buffalo hide while elongated gilded brass castors on the front legs fit like stockings. Books are stacked in an architectural bronze étagère with glass shelves.
*Photograph by Fritz von der Schulenburg*

best decorative schemes, the success lies in the details, be it a beautifully turned chair leg, an unusual moulding or the supplest hand-dyed leather.

Generosity of proportion is another hallmark: Lulu says that she will always prefer a handful of imposing statement pieces to a host of clutter, and aims to keep paring down each room until a simple, symmetrical balance is achieved. Antique textiles—from rare Isphahan carpets to fine central Asian embroideries—add colour and texture.

The nicest outcome of Soane Britain's advance into full-scale interior design is that bespoke pieces of furniture can go on to be made more widely available through the showroom. The "Blower" chair, for example, began life as a design for a private dining room at Bentley Motors' headquarters, and was inspired by the seats of a classic 1920s´ model.

Soane Britain owns a cabinet-making workshop in Dorset and relies on the skills of around 25 further studios in the UK, from metalsmiths to saddlers. Native craftsmanship is at the heart of the company's ethos: it's as ingrained as a seam of marble, and for all the growth and development that each new project brings, it is the one thing that will stay the same.

TOP LEFT:
A copy of a restrained Chippendale settee with generously scrolled arms invokes the 21st century when paired with a richly coloured 19th-century Susani.
*Photograph by Pearson Bruce*

BOTTOM LEFT:
A grand drawing room has a Russian family portrait over a monumental and sculptural new chesterfield by Soane. Its upholstering used more than 50 crimson goat skins, just as the 19th-century original would have.
*Photograph by Fritz von der Schulenburg*

FACING PAGE LEFT:
A version of a sculptural and exaggerated klismos chair, upholstered in toffee goatskin sits at a 1920s´ vellum and limed oak desk. The 19th-century painting of a bashi-bazouk is softly lit by a sculptural lamp carved from Jurassic stone.
*Photograph by Pearson Bruce*

FACING PAGE RIGHT:
A breakfast room with soft pink distemper walls has a beaten-iron stag-leg table supporting plaster rope lamps. Reflected in the early 20th-century painted mirror is a generously scaled Chinoiserie lantern with a verdigris finish.
*Photograph by James Moritmer*

# ANTONIA STEWART
## ANTONIA STEWART LTD

The best designers are the ones that never stop thinking about how they can make their clients' lives better. If Antonia Stewart finds the perfect antique chair for a Pimlico drawing room, two years after she has finished the project, she'll procure it nonetheless. Whatever she can't source she will design herself—so, for example, when some clients couldn't find exactly the right wallpaper, she simplified a textile pattern that they had liked, added spots to it, and then had it hand-made in the vibrant colours that the couple had requested: meticulous detail and effective creativity, hand in hand.

Antonia, who set up her own business in 2005 after seven years at Thorp Design, shares her studio with a similarly up-and-coming architectural practice, Studio DAR. They offer a slightly different approach, an integrated architectural and interior design service that gives clients the flexibility to buy into one or both disciplines, depending upon their requirements. This collaborative approach means that, right from the start, they are able to create an overall vision

LEFT:
A drawing room mixes contemporary details such as the limestone fireplace from Chesneys and grasscloth wall panelling with furniture from Dudgeon, JVB and William Yeoward. The room's elegance is heightened by the inclusion of antiques such as the 18th-century classical mirror, French ormolu clock and watercolours by David Roberts.
*Photograph by Edward Hill*

ABOVE TOP:
Rough-textured, twisted paper wallcovering and linen curtains create a comfortable setting in which to read or relax. Furniture and paintings are a mixture of new pieces and the client's own; the homeowner's great-grandfather was author John Buchan, whose writing desk is at the far end of the room.
*Photograph by Edward Hill*

ABOVE BOTTOM:
A contemporary and classic combination: a silvery shagreen wallpaper acts as a calm backdrop for two Georgian chests of drawers. Hand-stitched Swiss cushions decorate the bed and continue the red accenting. A modern ottoman covered in fabric by Ian Mankin provides extra storage.
*Photograph by Edward Hill*

FACING PAGE TOP:
The basement was opened up to create one large living space incorporating the kitchen and dining area. The full-height glass doors fold back along the long wall, enabling the kitchen and garden to work as one.
*Photograph by Edward Hill*

FACING PAGE BOTTOM:
The dining area is off-set from the kitchen space to give a separate eating area dominated by a large clock-face from a church in Provence, which has been set against a dark purple feature wall.
*Photograph by Edward Hill*

for the project, enabling them to develop the interiors schemes and the drawing package simultaneously.

Projects vary in size and location, from a Chelsea Harbour penthouse, a Grade I-listed John Nash house in Regent's Park, a family home in Gloucestershire, and beyond to international commissions. Clients may wish to source everything from new, but more often than not, Antonia is asked to incorporate specific pieces of existing furniture or art, something she tackles with characteristic relish.

Antonia works in a great range of styles, tailoring every project to its client. She describes her overall look as "Modern English", combining elements that are contemporary yet classic, individual yet international, and simple yet luxurious. Using a mixture of natural finishes—stone, timber, mother-of-pearl, polished plaster, mosaics, leathers, glass and steel—she builds up the hard finishes first to create a neutral backdrop, which she then softens with layers of textured fabrics. Colour, and her love of unexpected contrasts—a Steinway piano in front of a fibre-optic curtain, for example, or a French antique clock-face in a sleek London kitchen with a resin floor and cold cathode lighting—are trademarks of her look.

With a fascination for how things are made, Antonia ensures that she and her team take time to visit craftsmen's workshops to discover all they can about how things are actually manufactured. Understanding this, and realising where a product's limitations lie, enables design boundaries to be pushed when the need arises. With eyes permanently open to new inspirations, Antonia's infectious enthusiasm cannot help but rub off on her clients, just as it does on the unique homes she designs.

# GAIL TAYLOR
# KAREN HOWES
## TAYLOR HOWES DESIGNS LTD

Staying ahead of the curve is a challenging aspect of any job, but it's something that Gail Taylor and Karen Howes have nothing to worry about: as deadlines approach for the glossy magazines' new-year trend predictions, the founders of Taylor Howes Designs are on every journalist's speed-dial. Their enviable reputation for crystal-ball-gazing is the result of more than 17 years of hard work, a passion for design and finally—the magic ingredient—a solid friendship that continues to thrive.

Shaping this reputation is Taylor Howes Designs' extensive work on the show-apartments and houses of the most prestigious new developments in London. It provides a unique opportunity not only to plan a scheme two or three years in advance, but to create something edgy and imaginative. This feeds into the company's residential work, but with the important added considerations of practicality and longevity: fashionable colours and textures

that are as fickle as the seasons are fine for developments, but Taylor Howes Designs aims for something far more future-proof for its private clients.

When they started in business together in 1991, the two friends—who were first introduced at a party—did absolutely everything themselves. Today they oversee 21 staff, including the design director, Sheila El Hadery, and creative director, Sandra Drechsler, who have both been with the company since the mid-1990s, a mark of stability that is reflected in Taylor Howes Designs' consistently slick and confident interiors.

ABOVE:
An overscale piece of art became the focal point in the living space of this apartment in Kensington.
*Photograph by Tim Evan Cook*

FACING PAGE:
A separate library area was created on a raised platform in this contemporary London show apartment.
*Photograph by Tim Evan Cook*

Gail and Karen say they have slightly different tastes, with Gail's softer, more organic style acting as a foil for Karen's more overt glamour. Both are passionate about detail, whether that means planning the space in an optimum way to suit the clients' needs, or using the best craftsmen possible to create high-quality furniture and fittings. Too often, Gail says, people run out of steam when decorating, and overlook the little things that give a polished and professional finish—the equivalent of getting all dressed up for a night out, but forgetting to add a necklace, scarf and handbag to complete the look. Such an attitude means that comfort is never sacrificed to pure aesthetics in a Taylor Howes Designs scheme: it may be perfectly proportioned, beautifully tailored and harness the latest technology, but you'll always be able to kick off your shoes and enjoy it.

Gail and Karen's position at the top of their game is assured: in 2006 Taylor Howes Designs was named Andrew Martin International Interior Designer of the Year, one of the highest accolades in the industry. They are certainly in a comfortable place, but refuse to look back—for them, the most exciting project is the one that's just around the corner.

TOP LEFT:
The acrylic antlers and feature wall in chocolate grass-paper create the quirky dining room's backdrop.
*Photograph by Tim Evan Cook*

BOTTOM LEFT:
Bold but beautiful, geometric prints enhance the playfulness of this family room.
*Photograph by Tim Evan Cook*

FACING PAGE LEFT:
Getting the scale of the furniture right was the challenge in this glamorous reception room.
*Photograph by Tim Evan Cook*

FACING PAGE RIGHT:
Contemporary art and classic furnishings adorn this elegant home.
*Photograph by Tim Evan Cook*

# PHILIPPA THORP
## PHILIPPA THORP DESIGN LTD

Everyone knows that major house renovations usually equal major headaches, but Philippa Thorp can smooth over the roughest of problems. Her clients know it, too: one couple signed off the plans for their new home and embarked on a world tour while she worked her magic, such was their faith that she would get everything just right. They trust her because she gives each project her all; treating it with the same care as if it were her own home, and never stinting on quality of execution.

Philippa Thorp Design's extensive portfolio of exceptional work is one reason that the company inspires such confidence, but it's the physical make-up of the business that is the real secret to its success. Headed by Philippa, a whirlwind of energy and activity, the team of 12 includes architects, interior architects and interior designers, all working together for a common cause. In typical problem-solving style, Philippa brought the architecture side on board after she found herself frustrated by the lack of

LEFT:
With panoramic views of London, this apartment is ideal for entertaining.
*Photograph by Hufton and Crow*

synergy between her team and any external architects. She says she looks for free-thinkers when hiring an architect—someone creative as well as technical, who can paint a beautiful landscape as well as design a great building. The result of having such a coherent team is the perfect marriage between the building itself, the space within it and the client's lifestyle.

Architecture is Philippa's great passion: she realised—too late— that she should have studied the subject at university, and instead dropped out of a fashion and textiles degree to move to London. A temping job at Citibank led to a five-year stint in its marketing department, until a friend asked her to go into partnership in an interior design business. She was supposed to be the business brains of the outfit, but was so good at the design side that she switched to a creative role, learning as she went—by far the best way to do it, she maintains.

Philippa says she really got started on her career in the womb: her father was a gifted amateur artist and she spent her childhood visiting country houses and the cultural capitals of Europe. She confesses to a lifelong weakness for buying art, and speaks in artistic metaphors, too, likening each interior to a painting, completely unique. They are indeed unique: Philippa Thorp Design has a reputation for coming up with clever

RIGHT:
This staircase was designed to allow uninterrupted views of London.
*Photograph by Hufton and Crow*

FACING PAGE:
The floating staircase creates a cocoon for sitting.
*Photograph by Hufton and Crow*

solutions to the toughest problems, and the company has done it all. Certain ideas and schemes regularly capture the imagination of the press, including a giant teak bath seating 10—to make it, the company tracked down the holder of the record for hand-turning the world's largest wooden bowl. An innovative underground car-lift for the same house, based on a design for an aircraft carrier lift, was nominated for an international civil engineering award, coming a more-than-respectable second to the Copenhagen metro system.

These projects would not be possible without putting precision and technical skill at the heart of everything the company does. It takes at least six weeks on a new project to get initial ideas to flow, sketching and re-sketching them until they are just right, before an incredibly detailed drawing package shapes the final scheme—all before any work has been done on-site. Philippa Thorp Design doesn't shy away from doing things the hard way

TOP LEFT:
Whether for working or relaxing, this lounge offers a perfect atmosphere for any activity.
*Photograph by Chris Gascoigne*

BOTTOM LEFT:
Curvilinear elements within the kitchen make for a sociable space.
*Photograph by Martin Black*

FACING PAGE:
London by night serves as the perfect backdrop for any evening soirée.
*Photograph by Chris Gascoigne*

if it gets the right result. For this penthouse duplex, part of the concrete floor was cut away to create room for the new staircase: structurally, a complicated plan, but resulting in a dramatic feature that makes the most of the apartment's breathtaking views across London. The duplex is a perfect expression of the couple's lifestyle, with an open-plan look and bags of entertaining space, and—as with most projects—the majority of the fittings, furniture and accessories are all custom-made.

Philippa demands excellence from everyone she works with, and sets the bar pretty high herself, admitting that she is a complete perfectionist: she is wary of expanding her business any further, not just because it means taking one eye off the creative side, but because her current team works so brilliantly together. Whether the next project is a slick, tailored modern apartment or a rambling country house, Philippa retains an unqualified curiosity about how buildings work and, more importantly, how she can make them work even better for those who live in them.

ABOVE:
Captured from the comfort of the bath is a direct view of the London Eye.
*Photograph by Chris Gascoigne*

FACING PAGE:
A screen of joinery creates a wall between the bedroom and bathroom.
*Photograph by Chris Gascoigne*

# CAROLYN TREVOR
## CAROLYN TREVOR DESIGN

Architects and interior designers can make uneasy bedfellows—both vying to realise a creative vision that might not necessarily be mutual—but at Carolyn Trevor Design, there is no such professional tension. A trained architect herself, Carolyn has set up an interior design practice that complements the work of Trevor Lahiff Architects, the practice she runs with her husband Pat Lahiff: same office, same ideas, and no disharmony.

Beyond the obvious benefit for clients—only having one person to deal with in the often long and complex business of shaping a new home—it also means a creative coherence and an approach to interior design that is as precise as you would expect from someone with an architectural background. The company's drawing packages are so detailed, in fact, that they outsource the more routine work to Asia: it simply wouldn't be cost-effective to spend so much time working on them in London.

Carolyn's superior draughtsmanship was embedded during nearly a decade working on and off for renowned residential expert John Stefanidis. His practice has a reputation not just for being one of the hardest working in the business, but the most prestigious—her time there included a two-year spell living on a Welsh hillside while the team worked on the interiors for a major country house nearby. Setting up on her own in 1997, Carolyn's architectural practice expanded to include interior design as well, either as stand-alone projects or in conjunction with the company's in-house architects.

ABOVE:
Mirrored wallpaper and bespoke mirrors create a whimsical ambience for a girl's bedroom. For a splash of colour, the vintage armchair is covered in pink velvet, while the dressing table is more conservative and Baroque-inspired.
*Photograph by Fritz von der Schulenburg*

FACING PAGE:
The Murano glass sun chandelier is accentuated by the warmth of the antique bronze wall finish as well as the bespoke rosewood sideboard and dining table with bronze detailing. Covered in Missoni fabric, the Italian chairs are circa 1950; the Italian wall lights and mirror are of the same period.
*Photograph by Fritz von der Schulenburg*

Luxury residential interiors are the company's stock-in-trade, with a particular bent towards generous family homes—existing or new-build—that are no less stylish for their practicality. Each home is naturally dictated by each client's desires, but with a recognisable pared-down coherence that makes them relaxing spaces to inhabit. Furniture is often specially designed, to ensure the highest quality finish, complemented by antique pieces and the clients' own possessions. Bathrooms have become something of a speciality, often with seamless expanses of tailored marble—opulent, without seeming excessive.

Carolyn says she doesn't have a professional philosophy, other than to keep pushing onwards until she gets where she wants to be. After more than 10 years running her own business she is no less ambitious about the future, and still feels that there is more to achieve, including a move into commercial work—hotels, restaurants and bars—that will enable her to put an even more individual stamp on interiors. With 20-plus staff employed, she aspires not necessarily to grow larger, but to go deeper into design, creating spaces that are intensely suitable for their purpose, with comfort at their heart.

TOP LEFT:
The chevron oak parquet flooring elegantly contrasts the stainless-steel island and the Lactea Compac quartz worktops. Designed by Trevor Lahiff Architects with Robert Timmons furniture, the kitchen is dominated by a large skylight.
*Photograph by Fritz von der Schulenburg*

BOTTOM LEFT:
Calacatta Oro marble and the mirrored bath surround create a certain sophistication. The polished nickel frame informs the vanity unit as well as the glass doors.
*Photograph by Fritz von der Schulenburg*

FACING PAGE:
A palette of midnight blue pervades the space, with the built-in bookcases and joinery, Robsjohn Gibbings armchair and leather inlay of the antique desk all in the same colour. The sofa is Danish from circa 1960, while the bespoke silk rug is a Neisha Crosland zebra design.
*Photograph by Fritz von der Schulenburg*

# BUNNY TURNER
# EMMA POCOCK
## TURNER POCOCK

Often quoted—but no less true for that—William Morris's design doctrine, "have nothing in your houses that you do not know to be useful, or believe to be beautiful," strikes a deep chord with Bunny Turner and Emma Pocock. Their interior design company, Turner Pocock, might be a baby compared to more established firms—it was set up in early 2007—but with such an ethos, it would be hard to go wrong, and so it has proved with their clients.

The killer combination of youthful energy and a serious professional edge has quickly seen Turner Pocock's portfolio grow fat with prestigious commissions. Bunny and Emma were friends before they became business partners, and share a sense of humour and fun that's proved just as important as their mutual aesthetic tastes. From being able to laugh about things even when the going gets tough, to enveloping each client in a cloud of enthusiasm, they are determined to make every step of the design process as spirited as possible.

LEFT:
The drawing room's scheme maintains a modern focus while working around a set of existing antique Italian mirrors.
*Photograph by Sean Myers*

While Emma's career path is a fairly well-trodden one for an interior designer—after a degree in fashion design she trained at the KLC School of Design before working in-house for respected names such as Henrietta Spencer-Churchill and Kate Bingham—Bunny's background is more unorthodox. A postgraduate degree in contemporary art from the Courtauld Institute, followed by four years at a high-end commercial gallery, means that she more than has her finger on the pulse of London's art scene, experience that has proved invaluable when it comes to sourcing. Consequently, Bunny and Emma's schemes often use contemporary art as a focus and a starting point, and they can also offer advice on building up a collection, much as a

ABOVE LEFT:
A teenage girl's room scheme was designed to grow with her through the years; the space can be used as both a bedroom and a sitting room.
*Photograph by Sean Myers*

ABOVE RIGHT:
This bedroom scheme was built around the vibrant colours of a large, bright Natasha Law painting.
*Photograph by Sean Myers*

FACING PAGE TOP:
Two bespoke shagreen chests stand in front of custom-designed antique mirrored recesses on either side of the master bed. An interplay of textures is explored through silk-covered walls, a fur throw and luxurious velvets.
*Photograph by Sean Myers*

FACING PAGE BOTTOM LEFT:
A contemporary sculpture stands on an antique pietra dura tabletop, juxtaposing old and new as desired by the client.
*Photograph by Sean Myers*

FACING PAGE BOTTOM RIGHT:
A Cubist head by Kim James sits on a chest of drawers beside the master bed, complementing and continuing the theme started in the fragmented mirror.
*Photograph by Sean Myers*

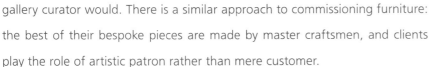

gallery curator would. There is a similar approach to commissioning furniture: the best of their bespoke pieces are made by master craftsmen, and clients play the role of artistic patron rather than mere customer.

Turner Pocock designs spaces that have dramatic tension, created by the contrast between structural, architectural purity and contemporary shape and colour. Formal and informal elements play off one another; ornate antiques provide a counterpoint to unpatterned surfaces. Bunny and Emma place high importance on the interplay of interesting textures, such as grasscloth walls, and on using high-quality, individually designed rugs that are almost as much works of art as those on the walls. All this is delivered with great surety, and a feeling that the journey has been just as satisfying as the finished result.

ABOVE LEFT:
A grid of works by the photographer Nick Hughes—brilliantly displaying night scenes of Kensington Gardens—was an attractive way of working with the double-height space.
*Photograph by Sean Myers*

ABOVE RIGHT:
Attention to detail is as important as the big picture—beautiful nickel and glass front door furniture sets the tone before entering the house.
*Photograph by Sean Myers*

FACING PAGE TOP:
An unusual loft space for a bachelor in a Victorian school conversion in Battersea included all the toys—from a purple pool-table to a seven-square-metre cinema screen.
*Photograph by Sean Myers*

FACING PAGE BOTTOM:
The open-plan space and double-height ceiling required careful thought to the way each area would be used. Zoning the areas broke up the space while keeping the living areas cosy.
*Photograph by Sean Myers*

# ROSE UNIACKE
## ROSE UNIACKE

Interiors are often said to be successful because of the unseen—the miles of cable that power hi-tech systems, or the deep thought that goes into how every space will be used—and in the same way, it is sometimes what has been omitted from a room that makes it work. It takes courage to leave things deconstructed and to let space breathe, allowing what is already in place to truly have its say, and this idea is the foundation stone of Rose Uniacke's style.

It carves a confident path between a Modernist desire to distil everything down to its purist form, and a parallel need for beauty and comfort in everyday life. Hard surfaces meet soft; furniture and fittings from every age are married; and pattern is downplayed in favour of an overall balance of textures and volumes. Enhancing the understatement is the use of natural materials such as timber, linen, silk and wool—textures that create the feeling of a well-loved, well-used home.

LEFT:
Woven and knitted cashmere rugs are draped across chairs in a London drawing room to add a bit of texture and interest. Bright walls are contrasted by the black and white contemporary photographs by Koudelka and Sugimoto. Parquet floors reclaimed from County Hall add a unique layer to the room's collection of 20th-century furniture, which includes a prominent drawing by Matthew Carr.
*Photograph by Andreas von Einsiedel*

Rose's Pimlico Road showroom reflects this sensibility. With unusual decorative antiques and self-designed pieces based on favourite finds, it presents the same coherent approach, giving customers the impression that they have just stepped into the impeccably styled home of a particularly tasteful friend. It also sells Rose's signature range of woven and knitted cashmere, borne from her frustration at not being able to find the perfect cashmere blanket—something that was beautifully but subtly finished, and could be draped to the floor over a double bed. In neutral tones that chime with virtually anything, they add unmitigated luxury to her schemes.

ABOVE:
A London drawing room's furniture pairs well with a simple yet inviting fireplace. The contrast between light chairs and dark cabinet pieces adds a unique dimension to the room's texture and presentation.
*Photograph by Andreas von Einsiedel*

FACING PAGE LEFT AND RIGHT:
Keeping within simple, inviting parameters for a London kitchen, a bright dining table contrasts with the dark cabinetry.
*Photographs by Andreas von Einsiedel*

The showroom is a stone's throw from her mother's shop, Hilary Batstone, from where Rose first started out before moving to her own premises. A firm favourite among fellow decorators, Rose would style it according to her own taste, with beautiful mirrors, crystal chandeliers and interesting 19th- and 20th-century furniture, and it proved so appealing that people wanted the full look in their own homes.

Although her own preferences err towards a muted palette— perfect for setting off contemporary art or modest furniture— ultimately each house defines its own style. As well as London homes and some collaborative work with a Los Angeles-based interior designer, she has also created schemes for country houses, including Mount Stuart on the Isle of Bute, a colour-saturated, Gothic Revival jewel. Town or country, the same spare approach applies to every interior: everything is just plentiful enough. Rose's work acts like a spirit level, finding just the right balance and restoring natural order.

RIGHT:
A master bathroom has found a piece of luxury with a fireplace and large bath. The cupboards were covered in painted linen and contribute a softer texture to the space.
*Photograph by Andreas von Einsiedel*

FACING PAGE LEFT AND RIGHT:
An elegant master bedroom contains a woven cashmere blanket upon the bed, a goatskin rug beneath the sitting chairs and a Hiroshi Sugimoto photograph above the covered headboard.
*Photographs by Andreas von Einsiedel*

# SHAILJA VOHORA
# SANJAY SHARMA
## INTERIORS WITH ART LTD

There's a strong family ethic at work at Interiors with Art. Brother and sister Sanjay Sharma and Shailja Vohora grew up surrounded by beauty, art and culture, and now they share that perspective with their clients. The company's elegant, bespoke homes are created from the ground up—from the first design inspiration, through to complex building and installation, to sourcing exquisite art and luxurious textiles. The foundation stone of every scheme, and the company's true strength, is Sanjay and Shailja's partnership.

For Interiors with Art, detailed attention to a client's lifestyle and personality is paramount. A contemporary Mayfair penthouse, a Louis XVI-style palace in the Middle East and a relaxed beach house in Spain will all be designed exclusively for each homeowner, and be based around his or her exact requirements.

Sanjay and Shailja attribute their passion for all things aesthetic to their mother, a talented artist and designer, and both siblings have grown up to become collectors themselves. With their multi-domicile upbringing—in India, East Africa, the US and the UK—they also have a particular insight into the finer points of how clients from different cultures want to live, a perspective that is increasingly important for a city with as much of an international countenance as London.

ABOVE:
With far-reaching views over Hyde Park Corner, this Mayfair penthouse includes a contemporary twist in its dining room, where antique chairs are covered in silver leather, sitting upon a cowhide rug.
*Photograph by Steve Stevens*

FACING PAGE:
Inlaid walnut and oak flooring, panelled walls and an eclectic mix of modern textures are integrated into a double reception space. Antique pieces, exquisite crystal and silver accessories and stunning art works complete the room.
*Photograph by Steve Stevens*

With 20 years' experience as an interior designer, Shailja leads on the creative side of the business. She is an alumna of the Inchbald School of Design, but with a deep interest in philosophy, history, art and culture, her personal and professional interests lie well beyond interior design. Having also studied at Christie's, Sotheby's and the School of Oriental and African Studies, she is an expert on the fine and decorative arts from all over the world, and this expansive knowledge comes into play in every interior. Such a background also adds a great deal of credence when dealing with clients who have their own collections, or who look to Interiors with Art to create homes with an artistic authenticity.

Sanjay, meanwhile, runs the business and logistics side with faultless precision, ensuring that each project comes to fruition on time and to budget. A management graduate from Pittsburgh's Carnegie Mellon University, his wealth of project management experience is the perfect complement to Shailja's design talents. Interiors with Art's "family" extends to the company's five designers and an in-house building team that is 30-strong and growing. Shailja and Sanjay make sure that everyone is there to see and celebrate each finished home, encouraging even higher standards for the next project, as well as fostering a strong sense of loyalty.

TOP LEFT:
Hand-stitched leather sliding panels, a Murano chandelier, ebonised dining table, satin curtains and mohair end-chairs on a smoked-oak floor deliver a sophisticated solution to this central London pied-à-terre kitchen.
*Photograph by Steve Stevens*

BOTTOM LEFT:
Precision planned for efficiency, stainless-steel appliances were incorporated into the design of this Bulthaup kitchen.
*Photograph by Steve Stevens*

FACING PAGE TOP:
Silk fabric walling, a bespoke Macassar ebony and suede headboard and Macassar side tables harmoniously sit within a Mayfair master bedroom. Hand-blown glass and silver lamps, an old gold commode, a shagreen and cashmere armchair and silk Versace bed linens all rest upon on a textured hand-tufted wool carpet.
*Photograph by Steve Stevens*

FACING PAGE BOTTOM:
A rich mahogany bar, shagreen and ebony gaming table and leather-framed sofas with slub silk upholstery add a definitive ambience. With views overlooking a private internal garden, this Mayfair reception room is complemented by an antique Asian rug punctuated with alpaca and cashmere throws; signed Picasso prints in hand-finished silver leaf frames complete the room.
*Photograph by Steve Stevens*

...

Beautiful bespoke joinery, the latest technology and handcrafted furniture are strong features of Interiors with Art's work, and Shailja and Sanjay will scan the globe to source the best products, be it Italian leather, South American silver, semi-precious stonework or the finest silks and embroideries. Shailja's passion for art and textiles provides a unique trademark, however: the siblings' embroidery workshop in India crafts fabrics for each project, from modern-looking appliquéd suede and leather to recreations of traditional Ottoman designs that can take months to make. Using hand-dyed threads and vegetable pigments results in textiles that are warm and delicate, blending seamlessly with both traditional and contemporary schemes.

The detailed planning that goes on behind-the-scenes may be invisible to clients, but they are the most important part of the job. Interiors with Art uses a comprehensive inventory system that tracks and records every item down to the last curtain tassel—so if a piece of textile hasn't left India to get to an upholsterer in the UK, it's instantly recognised and remedied. With business being done across several time-zones, it saves time, and leaves the designers to get on with what they do best—creating a perfect, totally individual new home for every client.

TOP RIGHT:
A silver-leafed domed ceiling and bespoke hand-blown chandelier are suspended above a Macassar ebony dining table and chairs; hand-embroidered panels and cushions surround. This Mayfair townhouse's dining room also includes a silk rug with leather binding, polished plaster walls and soft kidskin panelled chimney breast with mirrored television.
*Photograph by Steve Stevens*

BOTTOM RIGHT:
A ribbon mahogany centre table anchors a first-floor drawing room. Hanging beside polished plaster walls, silk curtains were designed with hand-embroidered leading along with silk and crystal passementerie. Silk mohair and pleated velvet upholstery define the sofas that intermingle with a crocodile leather bench; ripple sycamore arm chairs are skillfully presented with kidskin leather and hand-embroidered, appliquéd and beaded cushions.
*Photograph by Steve Stevens*

FACING PAGE:
Bamboo and silver-leaf wallpaper is paired with walnut floors, both of which serve as stunning accents around a bespoke walnut and mahogany dining table. Bespoke silver-leaf and stained-oak cabinets with Murano glass lamps, an embossed, faux-suede centre table with polished French nailing and zebra-print hair on hide stools give this double reception space a charming look. Concluding this dramatic central London room are cut velvet cushions on moiré silks and velvet upholstery with art works by Miro and Dali.
*Photograph by Steve Stevens*

# TINA WEAVER
## TINA WEAVER INTERIOR DESIGN

When Tina Weaver talks about the importance of good lighting, you can feel her passion for design. She was brought up in the Arctic city of Tromsø in Norway, where for three months of the year the sun never rises—so she knows a thing or two about maximising the natural light in even the gloomiest of rooms. Mirrors on a grand scale and intelligent lighting are a couple of her techniques for turning ordinary spaces into sparkling retreats from the busy world, but they are just one tool in a multifaceted toolbox.

Tina came to the UK in 1996 to study at London's KLC School of Design, a relationship that continues to bear fruit today, since she now teaches there on a consultancy basis. It's not merely a job: the experience of working with like-minded people from many different backgrounds, all sharing their creative passions, helps to keep her own work fresh and interesting.

Designed to appeal to as many senses as possible, Tina's schemes have depth and comfort, and are always inviting. She says it's probably her Scandinavian background that would never allow her to stray too far from an essential simplicity, but her work is far from plain: it just means that symmetry is the general rule, for example, or that colour may be used in smaller doses, but it is nonetheless vital and invigorating. Generously scaled furniture adds visual impact, and there are always a few focal points and surprises—a single stand-out antique piece, or a specially commissioned painting—to catch the eye.

ABOVE:
A dining room with an amazing view of London offers a glimpse of Tower Bridge. Curvy chairs and a reflecting table enhance the experience when the homeowners are entertaining.
*Photograph by Jens Juncker-Jensen*

FACING PAGE:
A small entrance was significantly altered to create a stunning first impression. The use of mirrors, light strips in the coving and the opening up of a doorway towards the living room made it feel twice the size.
*Photograph by Jens Juncker-Jensen*

A magician-like ability to conjure up extra space is another trademark, one that is especially highly prized by London clients. It sometimes requires the complete re-think of a layout, by opening up hallways to make a bright and welcoming entrance area, for example, but it could equally mean the use of clever bespoke cabinetry that's both visually appealing and unobtrusive at the same time.

Tina's first piece of advice to anyone designing for themselves is to create a lighting plan well before any actual decorating takes place, in order to fully take advantage of the wonderful—but often complex—technology that can transform ordinary space. Floors can be washed with illumination from hidden strips at the base of a wall; unusual chandeliers can bounce brilliant droplets off windows and mirrors. She also loves using oversized furniture and objects for impact and surprise, preferring to use a few imposing pieces

rather than a scattering of smaller ones. The overarching theme, however, is beauty and practicality in equal amounts: not just a way to describe the perfect lighting scheme, or a really interesting piece of furniture, but Tina's entire decorating philosophy, too.

ABOVE LEFT:
A narrow hallway incorporates a slimline console table and lamp to give some ambience when entering the flat; an oversized vase sits on the landing.
*Photograph by Ole S. Hansen*

ABOVE RIGHT:
The console table was made from compressed stone and had down-lights built in to it. The painting was commissioned and made by artist Cheryl Hayeem.
*Photograph by Ole S. Hansen*

FACING PAGE TOP:
A Boston ivy was planted outside the bedroom and over time it has draped itself around the window to form beautiful natural curtains.
*Photograph by Ole S. Hansen*

FACING PAGE BOTTOM:
An otherwise calm bedroom was made more lively with the use of sensual red highlights. The soft fabrics were all inspired by roses.
*Photograph by Ole S. Hansen*

# MELISSA WYNDHAM

## MELISSA WYNDHAM LTD

Even though she has worked on some of the grandest country houses in Britain, Melissa Wyndham believes that any space at all can be made to look wonderful, no matter how modest or unattractive it started out. She cheerfully admits that half the time, people simply have their furniture in the wrong place: a few tweaks, and she's created something infinitely more liveable, with not a penny spent.

It helps, of course, if clients already have great collections of furniture and art, and interesting historic buildings in which to keep them, but nonetheless there's a great skill in being able to instantly visualise the optimum level of comfort and style that can be achieved in any interior. Melissa has this skill in spades, and she always tries to subtly encourage clients to be more daring or experimental—to move away from lifeless historical recreations or uniform taupe boxes and explore something that's much more exciting and personal.

Melissa has quite the best grounding in interior design it's possible to have— her great-aunt was Nancy Lancaster, founder of Colefax and Fowler and one of the most eminent taste-makers of the 20th century. However, she spent a long time studiously avoiding the family business, thinking she ought to try something different. When some years later, she did take a job working for a London interior designer, she realized her mistake: decorating was for her after all.

ABOVE:
French toile was chosen as the wallcovering because the homeowners sought a cosy yet restrained ambience. The only picture in the room is an 18th-century French grisaille portrait.
*Photograph by Gavin Kingcome*

FACING PAGE:
Antique furniture and modern British paintings combine in this Chelsea drawing room. The blue and white lamp base is 1960s' ceramic; the fabric on the sofa is by Raoul Textiles.
*Photograph by Gavin Kingcome*

A childhood infused with memories of her Aunt Nancy's homes, which in an era of post-war austerity were always elegant and comfortable without being showy, has created a lasting legacy. A tailored finish with a certain informality are Melissa's hallmarks, whether the space is traditional or contemporary. Antiques have a large part to play in this look, but she is no elitist—rather than going for the rarest or most expensive items, she seeks out objects with an individual aesthetic quality, from any era, that will perfectly match the personality of the space. Things must "go" but not match, so that everything appears effortless.

With a keen understanding of texture, pattern and colour, Melissa also designs rugs for Robert Stephenson, borne out of frustration that she couldn't find modern floor-coverings that she liked. In fact, with their muted palette and simple graphic designs, one of their strengths is that they blend with almost anything, and the same can be said of her textile range. It

pleases her best not when a client decides to use her products, but when other decorators use her work, as if it's somehow the proof—not that it's needed—that she's doing everything just right.

ABOVE:
A Regency fireplace was reinstated as a focal point on the blank chimney breast. A late-18th-century Italian mirror and draperies made with Christopher Moore fabric complement the setting.
*Photograph by Gavin Kingcome*

FACING PAGE TOP LEFT:
The Bessarabian kilim from Robert Stephenson pulls the room together even though the colours are not a perfect match.
*Photograph by Gavin Kingcome*

FACING PAGE BOTTOM LEFT:
Finished with a late-Regency English bed and a 20th-century French mirror, the bedroom has blue and white printed linen walls that foster a restful atmosphere. The unusual shelves came from the Nancy Lancaster sale and are probably Dutch.
*Photograph by Gavin Kingcome*

FACING PAGE RIGHT:
Covered in green ottoman fabric, the unique high-backed chair came from a junk shop in Berkshire. A Bohemian glass jar—one of a pair sits on top of the chimneypiece. The sisal rug gives the room an informal feel.
*Photograph by Gavin Kingcome*

# TINO ZERVUDACHI
## MLINARIC, HENRY & ZERVUDACHI LTD

Most decorators pride themselves on their chameleon-like ability to reinvent their aesthetic to suit a client's needs, but few companies have such an all-encompassing portfolio as Mlinaric, Henry & Zervudachi. From homes that are spare and minimal to those which are lavish and ornate, via showrooms, museums and galleries, there is no space that is beyond its capabilities.

Mlinaric, Henry & Zervudachi has one of the most impressive pedigrees of any interior design firm in London, and with a second principle office in Paris and small satellite offices in New York and Tokyo, its reputation is a global one. Initially an alliance forged in the late 1960s by David Mliniaric and Hugh Henry, the company acquired its present name when Tino Zervudachi became a partner in 1986. It continues to evolve, with Tino, now at the creative helm, dividing his time between London and Paris—and with Hugh Henry

and Jason Roberts in London, and Kelly Wilde, Dennis Pyle and Antoine de Sigy in Paris.

This two-centred approach has its creative benefits: the company has access to the best of everything, be that French textiles or English vibrancy, and the two studios can be flexible about whether they work separately or collaboratively on individual projects. Tino's eponymous gallery, in Paris's exclusive Palais Royal arcade, is the perfect expression of his egalitarian approach to decorating, with its displays of museum-quality antiques

ABOVE:
A very large circular mirror from the 1950s reflects an interesting mix of 20th-century and contemporary styles; the room is complemented by a rug designed by Tino Zervudachi.
*Photograph by Marianne Haas*

FACING PAGE:
An 18th-century English crystal chandelier hangs over a seat designed by Tino Zervudachi. Two 1940s' gilded tables sit in front of a Tino Zervudachi-designed green mohair velvet embossed mahogany sofa.
*Photograph by Marianne Haas*

alternating with shows of contemporary paintings, photography, sculpture and furniture.

The company's reputation was originally built upon David Mlinaric's skilled manipulation of historic houses, primarily in period style, but has since broadened its scope—more excitement can be achieved from boldly mixing up old and new. Tino has little interest in quick-fix developments where no thought has been given to proportion or practicality. In every project, he says that he looks for the essence of a particular space, and works from there: an innate sympathy with the architecture is crucial, and it's the only real rule. Despite the mix of natural textures and a fine-tuned colour sense, a certain

restraint means that this essential character is always the first thing to be noticed, which makes for homes that are both uncontrived and welcoming.

The sheer variety of work that the company undertakes is the very thing that clients are attracted to, concludes Tino: they know that they are not going to be fobbed off with a house style, rather that they will be listened to and understood. It certainly takes bravura to be able to pull off a Tuscan castle, a modern London apartment and a compact Parisian pied-à-terre, but behind that bravura are decades of skill and knowledge combined with a passion for new ideas.

ABOVE LEFT:
Within this 18th-century drawing room, contemporary designs combine with the historically reproduced mirror and chairs and red-painted bookcases, adding warmth to the room.
*Photograph by Marianne Haas*

ABOVE RIGHT:
Among its many attributes, this 19th-century conservatory displays a mix of 18th-century French furniture and contemporary art with a tented blind ceiling.
*Photograph by Marianne Haas*

FACING PAGE:
An Arts-and-Crafts kitchen was made from a warren of smaller rooms, adding beams to the ceiling and original 19th-century William Morris fabric curtains.
*Photograph by Marianne Haas*

# SPECTACULAR HOMES OF LONDON

**LONDON TEAM**
GROUP PUBLISHER: Guy MacNaughton
GRAPHIC DESIGNER: Jonathan Fehr
EDITOR: Emily Brooks
PRODUCTION COORDINATOR: Laura Greenwood

**HEADQUARTERS TEAM**
PUBLISHER: Brian G. Carabet
PUBLISHER: John A. Shand
EXECUTIVE PUBLISHER: Phil Reavis
DIRECTOR OF DEVELOPMENT & DESIGN: Beth Benton Buckley
DIRECTOR OF BOOK MARKETING & DISTRIBUTION: Julia Hoover
PUBLICATION MANAGER: Lauren B. Castelli
SENIOR GRAPHIC DESIGNER: Emily A. Kattan
GRAPHIC DESIGNER: Ashley Rodges
GRAPHIC DESIGNER: Red Scofield
EDITORIAL DEVELOPMENT SPECIALIST: Elizabeth Gionta
MANAGING EDITOR: Rosalie Z. Wilson
EDITOR: Katrina Autem
EDITOR: Amanda Bray
EDITOR: Anita Kasmar
EDITOR: Ryan Parr
EDITOR: Daniel Reid
MANAGING PRODUCTION COORDINATOR: Kristy Randall
PRODUCTION COORDINATOR: Drea Williams
TRAFFIC COORDINATOR: Amanda Johnson
ADMINISTRATIVE MANAGER: Carol Kendall
ADMINISTRATIVE ASSISTANT: Beverly Smith
CLIENT SUPPORT COORDINATOR: Amanda Mathers
CLIENT SUPPORT ASSISTANT: Meghan Anderson

PANACHE PARTNERS, LLC
CORPORATE HEADQUARTERS
1424 Gables Court
Plano, TX 75075
469.246.6060
www.panache.com

# INDEX

# THE PANACHE COLLECTION

CREATING SPECTACULAR PUBLICATIONS FOR DISCERNING READERS

## Dream Homes Series
**An Exclusive Showcase of the Finest Architects, Designers and Builders**

Carolinas
Chicago
Coastal California
Colorado
Deserts
Florida
Georgia
Los Angeles
Metro New York
Michigan
Minnesota

New England
New Jersey
Northern California
Ohio & Pennsylvania
Pacific Northwest
Philadelphia
South Florida
Southwest
Tennessee
Texas
Washington, D.C.

## Spectacular Homes Series
**An Exclusive Showcase of the Finest Interior Designers**

California
Carolinas
Chicago
Colorado
Florida
Georgia
Heartland
London
Michigan
Minnesota
New England

New York
Ohio & Pennsylvania
Pacific Northwest
Philadelphia
South Florida
Southwest
Tennessee
Texas
Toronto
Washington, D.C.
Western Canada

## Perspectives on Design Series
**Design Philosophies Expressed by Leading Professionals**

Carolinas
Chicago
Colorado
Florida
Georgia
Minnesota

New England
Pacific Northwest
San Francisco
Southwest
Texas

## City by Design Series
**An Architectural Perspective**

Atlanta
Austin, Houston & San Antonio
Charlotte
Chicago
Dallas
Denver
Orlando
Phoenix
San Francisco

## Spectacular Wineries Series
**A Captivating Tour of Established, Estate and Boutique Wineries**

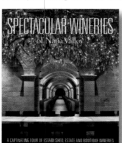

California Central Coast
Napa Valley
New York
Sonoma

## Art of Celebration Series
**The Making of a Gala**

Florida Style
New York Style
Washington, D.C. Style

## Speciality Titles

Distinguished Inns of North America
Extraordinary Homes California
London Homes

London Architects
Spectacular Golf of Colorado
Spectacular Golf of Texas

Spectacular Hotels
Spectacular Restaurants of Texas
Visions of Design

---

Panache Partners, LLC    1424 Gables Court    Plano, Texas 75075    469.246.6060    www.panache.com